◘

A FAITH THAT MAKES SENSE

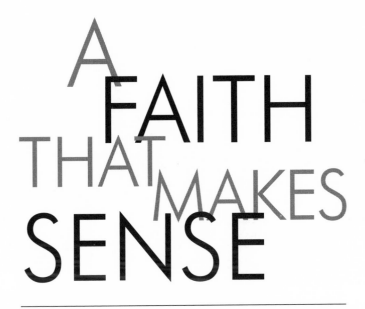

A FAITH THAT MAKES SENSE

REFLECTIONS FOR
PEACE, PURPOSE,
AND JOY

ROBERT J. CORMIER

A CROSSROAD BOOK
THE CROSSROAD PUBLISHING COMPANY
NEW YORK

The Crossroad Publishing Company
370 Lexington Avenue
New York, N.Y. 10017

Library of Congress Cataloging-in-Publication Data

Cormier, Robert J.
   A faith that makes sense : reflections for peace,
purpose and joy / Robert J. Cormier.
       p.   cm.
   ISBN 0-8245-1817-9
   1. Faith Meditations.   2. Christian life Meditations.
   I. Title.
   BV4637 .C63 1999
   234' .23—dc21
                                        99-33228
                                        CIP

1   2   3   4   5   6   7   8   9   10   03   02   01   00   99

CONTENTS

◘

CONTENTS

◼

CONTENTS

□

CONTENTS

◘

CONTENTS

◘

THOUGHTS FOR THE STRUGGLE

THE LIFE OF FAITH

CONTENTS

◪

CONTENTS

◼

◱

INTRODUCTION

A *Faith That Makes Sense* is a collection of reflections offered in hope of helping people grow in their peace, sense of purpose, and joy. The reflections can be read individually, by chapters, or, for a fairly complete adult spirituality, in order. The only way this book should not be read is backwards.

FAITH

◘

WHAT IS FAITH?

What is faith? In its most developed form, faith is a deeply personal relationship with God. In its simplest form, however, faith is the way we explain our life. Guided by what the human spirit has already decided, the simplest form of this explanation consists of the following three basic ideas:

Heaven: We exist because God, who does not need to be explained, decided to share His life.

Love: We are here, in this world, to participate in our own creation. God is giving each of us the opportunity to become our own person. This is the reason that we are born unformed, unknowing, and utterly self-centered, and we are called to grow. We are called to grow in the faith that inspires the love which makes us more like God, and prepares us to share God's life as richly as we might.

God's plan: In the act of creation, God put into action a plan for everything that would ever happen, including all the events of all of our lives. He did this knowing how we would respond to these events. In this way, we become the people God wants us to be, while, in the process, each of us still becomes our own person. ■

3

◙

THE GIFTS OF FAITH

Faith gives gifts. It is a way of understanding things that change the lives of those who possess it.

To believe in heaven frees us from the dread of death, or the need to keep ourselves distracted—never really living—because we cannot face the facts of life.

To believe in heaven frees us from anguish at the deaths of those we love. Though we may miss them, we know that they have gone to God and are more alive than we are. We also know that one day we will be reunited with them.

To believe in heaven lets us dream. Though all of us have our dreams, the day comes when most people have to admit, if only to themselves, that their dreams are not going to come true. This never happens to people of faith. We know that our dreams are going to come true, the only place they ever could.

Knowing that we were made for divine life, we understand that we were made to want divine life. Presumably, we also understand that no worldly thing could ever fill us. This is the reason that to get one thing is to want another. Therefore, though we can and we should work to make our lives and our world better, we need not suffer over any one thing we do not yet have.

We need not anguish over any one problem we have not yet solved. We need not feel envy.

Not seeking more from things than they can give, we can enjoy the things we do have. Our house does not have to be a heavenly mansion. Our house is not in heaven. But, if we find love there, it can still be a home. Our car does not have to make us important. A car makes no one important. If it starts, however, it can take us where we need to go. The people in our lives do not need to be perfect. No one is perfect. If, nonetheless, they are trying, they can still be our companions.

To believe in heaven gives us joy. At the very least, it gives us hope.

To believe in love gives us purpose. We know why we are here. We know what we should do. We know that what we do will make an eternal difference.

If we believe that we are here to grow in love, we love. We are free—free from the fear that we are giving more than others—to live the only kind of life that could ever satisfy us. God would not have made us so that we could ever be happy doing what is wrong. Rather, He made us so that we can be happy only when we are doing what is right. This is the reason that if we live selfishly we are never satisfied, no matter how much we have, whereas if we live a life of love we are always satisfied, no matter how little we have.

If to grow in faith and love is our goal, we gain control over our lives. We are always in a position to do what we want most of all. This is not true if fame or fortune is our goal. If something worldly is our goal, we have to hope that the world will cooperate. (Probably it will not.) If, instead, to grow in faith and love is our goal, we can always do what we want, no matter what the world may do. If something goes wrong, we can accept it, and thus our faith will grow. If people offend or disappoint us, we can forgive them, and thus our love will grow.

If we believe in God's plan, we have the best possible reason to accept ourselves for who we are. After all, God's plan for everything is also His plan for each of us. Right now, each of us is the person God has made us. Though we hope that we will continue to grow, we still know that so far our life has followed God's plan. Thus, we can forgive ourselves for what we cannot or did not do, or have done and cannot change. We no longer need to see ourselves through the eyes of others, or compare ourselves with others. Indeed, once we recognize that God has put all His love into our making, we can love ourselves for who He made us. This makes possible a sincere love of others.

To believe in God's plan allows us to accept whatever has happened and cannot be changed. We may not yet know why something hard had to happen, but we can still be confident that it happened for the best possible reason. Likewise, to believe in God's plan allows us to accept whatever is happening now and cannot yet be changed.

Since we know that everything that is going to happen—once it has happened and cannot be changed— will also follow God's plan, we can live our lives without fear of what may come. We can live without the impossible burden of thinking that everything depends on us. Everything does not depend on us. Everything depends on God. Our job is to do our best, the best we can right now. The rest is up to God and His plan.

To believe in God's plan gives us peace. ∎

□

THE GIFTS OF FAITH
ARE IMMEDIATE

Take, for example, a hundred dollar bill. It looks like a good thing. It looks like something anyone would want.

But why? Because we can use it to buy something that we want, that perhaps we need or can use, that perhaps will help us enjoy our life a little better, that perhaps will work for us tomorrow, perhaps.

Faith is so much more efficient. Faith brings with it the gifts—the effects on our spirit—we automatically, immediately receive if we really believe.

It gives the peace that we automatically, immediately receive if we really believe in God's plan.

It gives the purpose that we automatically, immediately receive if we really believe in love.

It gives the joy that we automatically, immediately receive if we really believe in heaven.

And without these gifts, no thing can help us be happy. ■

⊡

FAITH DOESN'T CHANGE THINGS, IT CHANGES HOW WE SEE THINGS

"**I**'m not losing a daughter; I'm gaining a son." It is often true. And what looked sad now looks good.

This is how faith works. It doesn't change things. It changes how we see things such that what looked bad now looks good, or at least better.

A problem becomes an opportunity for faith.

Another problem becomes an opportunity for love.

Another thing that we don't have, something we just see from a distance, is still information that can help us imagine what life with God will be like. ■

◘

WHAT IS THE "GOOD NEWS"?

God made us for life with Him.

God loves us, and all we need to do is love Him back.

God is working with us through everything He sends into our lives to prepare us for our life with Him.

———

Another way to put it:

God made us for life with Him.

God works with us through everything He sends into our lives to prepare us for our life with Him.

Our part: We only need to do our best. ■

FIVE STEPS
TO FAITH

◘

TRY

To get faith, first we need to try it. We need to ask ourselves the questions that faith answers, and see how we feel about the answers.

We begin with the most basic question of all:

Where do we come from? Is it possible that everything—the universe out there and also the universe within us—is just here, from nothing, for nothing, and is on its way *to* nothing? Or does it make more sense to us that the world and we were made, made by God?

So, why did God make us? Is it possible that we were made for death? Is it possible that we who were made to want life so desperately were given life so that life could be taken away? Or is it not evident that we were made for life, life with God who made us?

Why then are we here, in *this* world? Is it possible that we are here merely to kill time before we go to heaven? Or is it not obvious that we are here for something important? And what is more important than love? And by loving don't we grow in love, and in our likeness to God? And by becoming more like God, aren't we growing in our ability to share His life when finally we see Him face to face? And by this process, isn't God

13

giving us some responsibility for who we are, the chance to become our own person?

So, if what we do is so important, why do our lives depend on so much we cannot control? Is it possible that God put us here at the mercy of events that even He does not control, that He has left us here at the mercy of luck, or other people's badness, or even our own created weakness?

Another way to look at it: When God made the world, did He know what was going to happen? Did He care? If He did care, and He did know, and He did plan the events of our lives knowing how we would respond to them, wouldn't this make us the people He wants us to be while at the same time giving us a role in our own creation?

What do you think?

———

Why does to "try" faith reveal to us the truth? To try faith reveals the truth because God knew that we would hear about faith from many people, that most would seem sure, and that often they would contradict one another. Therefore, He knew that unless there were some way for us to see the truth for ourselves, faith would not be possible. For this reason, the truth of faith was written into human nature and will be recognized by anyone who looks for it in the right place.

How precisely do we look for the truth of faith? We ask ourselves the questions that faith answers and *consider the alternative.* ∎

◘

DECIDE

So often we are urged to "have faith," to "believe." Having faith and believing are spoken of as acts of the will. It is not, however, the human experience that we can believe because we want to. Indeed, when people do believe what they want to believe, we speak of it as bad. Therefore, the question is put to us: How is faith an act of the will? Is there anything we can do to have faith?

The answer is yes; we can decide. We can ask ourselves the questions that faith answers and decide what we think.

Unfortunately, we resist this decision. We also know that if we decide we do believe, we will have to live differently. We know that we will have to let people see that we believe. This is scary. It seems safer to hang on to a vague faith that asks for little. The problem is, a faith that asks little offers little. It does not give the gifts we get if we really believe.

Therefore, we need to decide. And how do we do that? We look at what faith says. We consider the alternative. We see what makes more sense.

Does it make sense that we are just here—yes or no?

Can it be that we were made for death—yes or no?

Is it imaginable that we are here to just kill time? Isn't growing in love what makes us greater—yes or no?

When God made the world, did He know what was going to happen—yes or no?

Since, in fact, the truth is clear, what stands in faith's way is our reluctance to decide, to take a stand, and to be faced with the need to live it out.

Of course, properly understood, faith offers so much more than it asks.

Look, see, decide.

———

Another reason we don't decide: We think we already have. We don't disbelieve so we think that we believe. We confuse hoping that something is true with thinking that something is true. The first takes nothing. The second takes decision. ■

◘

TRUST

Sometimes we are reluctant to decide about what we believe partly because we don't believe that we can know the truth. We know what we feel but we don't feel that we know. We don't feel sure about matters of faith. Still:

We feel, for sure, that the world has come from somewhere.

We cannot imagine that we were made for death.

We definitely feel that love is the way.

And we do feel that things happen for a reason. We can hardly feel otherwise.

What we do not realize is that these feelings *are* our knowledge of the truth. They are the response of our whole self to questions involving the whole of reality. This is how the truth of faith is supposed to be seen.

We can say this because these experiences are the best we have. They are the best that anyone has. They are surely telling us the truth. After all, God would not have put us here without the power to do what we are here for. We are here to grow in the love that prepares us for eternal life. We must have been given the ability to see the truth that makes this possible.

Trust—yourself. ■

◘

JUMP

Faith may begin as we ask ourselves the questions that faith answers, but the proof of faith is in the living. Living faith, we experience the superiority of a life that only faith makes sense of. Living faith provides the ultimate evidence that what we believe is true.

Herein lies a problem. In order to feel sure about our faith, we need to begin to live it before we feel sure. In this sense, we must just jump in.

What do we need to do? Actually, it's quite simple.

To vindicate our faith in heaven, we need to let go. We need to look at anything we thought we absolutely had to have and, in the name of our faith in heaven, acknowledge that we don't absolutely have to have it. This is not to say we don't want it, but now we acknowledge that we don't have to have it.

To vindicate our faith in love, we need to love. We need to do something for someone's else sake. We need to give and not worry about getting something in return. To do what is good and not worry whether anyone will notice. To do what is good because it is good.

To vindicate our faith in God's plan, we need to embrace, ourselves and our lives. We need to choose to be ourselves regardless of what others might think. We need to acknowledge what we regret, and accept it as our life. We need to say, "come what may," and mean it.

Just do it. Just jump in.

———

Another reason that faith needs to be lived in order to be had: To choose something, we must reject what contradicts it.

Everyone knows that you cannot bet on both sides in a game and win. To win you need to choose—for one and against another. We understand this when it comes to sports, but sometimes we miss it when it comes to faith.

We say we believe. We say we pray at home. We avoid the big sins.

But we never speak of our faith. We do not in any sense practice it. We give or serve as little as we can get away with. And if we can get it, or get more of it, we must.

Sometimes we are tempted by the idea that we are having the best of both worlds. In reality, what we have is the worst. With one foot in faith, we often feel guilty. But, with the other foot in the world, we still suffer over what we do not have, or what others might be thinking.

To gain from faith we have to choose it. This means that we have to unchoose what contradicts it. ■

◨

NOW

Since faith involves sacrifice and even risk, the time for faith is never now. We can always find some reason not to do what is risky, especially if there is no one to force us and, because others would rather not be challenged, society tells us not to.

The time for faith is now. Therefore we must make it now. We must recognize that no other time is coming, and that only our decision can give us the greater life we seek.

If what we seek is a greater life, why not now? If not now, when?

———

We need faith now because if we wait until something terrible happens, it may be too late.

When something terrible has happened, we become upset. Often we become too upset to consider the questions that faith answers. We have had no chance to live the answers out. We have had no time to become accustomed to a whole new way of looking at life.

In contrast, if we have already done the basic work that goes into believing, if we have already become accustomed to faith's way of looking at life, when we need it we will have it. Faith will work for us when we need it because it worked for us when we didn't.

Faith: *You need it before you need it.* ■

MORE
ABOUT
BELIEVING

◘

CREATION WAS SIGNED

Tonight, when you go to bed, before you fall asleep, when it is dark and quiet and there are no distractions, think about the simple fact that you are alive. Say to yourself "I am"—not "I am this or I am that" but simply "I am"—and think about what you mean when you say it.

Immediately you will realize that you are much more than you can possibly put into words. You can say certain things *about* you, but what you *are*, what you are as a person, is much too much to put into words.

In this same moment, you will realize that you are much too much just to be here. You could not have come from nothing, for nothing, and be headed to nothing. You must have come from somewhere.

This is human experience because, for all intents and purposes, creation was signed. Whenever you look closely at anything, you experience that it was made. This is God's signature on creation. Some say they can see it when they look at the majesty of the mountains. Others say they can see it when they look at the power of the sea. But you can even see the hand of God if you look at your own hand, not the fact that it works but the very fact that it is there. You can see the hand of God best when you look at the thing you know best—yourself.

———

Another way to have an experience of God: Close your eyes and concentrate on the present, the time which is passing *right now*. This is an effective way to put aside distractions, and to experience the richness of what it is to be alive, what it is to be a person. It is an effective way to experience the fact that there is more to existence than usually meets the eye. ■

◙

FROM NOTHING
NOTHING COMES

From nothing nothing comes. Therefore, if we experience even one moment of goodness in this world, we know that its maker is good.

If He is good, He has a good reason for anything else that might be happening, even if it doesn't look too good.

God being good, He must be using what is happening to prepare us for our life with Him. ∎

⊡

2 + 2 = 4

2 + 2 = 4. And we are sure about it.

We are less sure about something that is supposedly proved by a scientific experiment, even if we see it with our own eyes. But that's OK. We don't expect science to be math. Math is about definitions; science is about how reality functions. Therefore, we judge science by a different standard. And, according to that standard, we can still be confident that what we have discovered is true.

But this standard is useless for evaluating statements like "I love you." The human heart is much more complex than most of the things that science studies. Our belief that someone loves us is the judgment of our heart—our whole self. Therefore, we do not expect the truth of someone's love for us to look like math or science. Nonetheless, we can still be confident that we know whether someone loves us or not.

We can say the same about the truth of faith. As a judgment of our whole spirit about the meaning of the whole of reality, faith doesn't look like math or science. But that's OK. Given what we should expect, the truth of faith can still be clear.

Let us be clear about the point: Many of us suffer

doubt not because we don't know what we think but because we compare our sense of the truth of faith with our sense of other things we believe are true. This does not help. It is not fair. And it is not necessary. ∎

⊡

FAITH FULFILLS
OUR HUMAN NATURE

Faith offers hope, and purpose, and peace. Not to believe offers nothing.

Faith gives us the best life that we can possibly have. Not to believe restrains our joy.

Faith brings out the best in people. Not to believe makes no one better.

Faith fulfills our human nature. And this itself is a sign of the truth of faith.

———

To believe or not to believe is not like the choice between two loves, two jobs, or two places to live, both of which have wonderful qualities though different. These are choices between two good things. These are choices where to choose one good thing is to reject another, and to live with the question of whether we made the right decision.

Faith does not present us with such a choice. Faith offers hope, and purpose, and peace. Not to believe leads to hopelessness, meaninglessness, and misery.

Oh, it is true that faith must be lived out. But even here we are not presented with a choice between two good things.

Faith asks us to let go of the idea that there are

28

certain things we have to have. But not to let go does not mean that we get what we thought we had to have.

Faith asks us to love. But not to love does not give us a life that can satisfy.

Faith asks us to accept what God has sent. But not to accept things doesn't change them. Not to accept leaves us only with anger.

Faith is a better choice. ∎

◘

FAITH REQUIRES
NO COMPROMISE

Often we have to choose between quantity and quality, between something that tastes good or something that is good for us, between something that pays well or something that is less risky. Faith does not present us with such a choice.

Faith is a better life in every way. It is a better way to get to heaven. It is a better way to live here. It is better for individuals. It is better for society. It helps you when you're happy. It helps you when you're sad.

And this is yet another sign of the truth of faith. ■

◘

THE VIEW FROM ON HIGH

We pay attention to people who see from a high place, from the top of a tower or the top of a mountain. We understand that they have a special point of view, and we are therefore guided by what they tell us.

We can see something similar in the point of view of people of extraordinary faith. Not higher in a physical sense, they do have a higher (or deeper) point of view spiritually.

We know that they indeed have a higher (or deeper) point of view spiritually because their lives show it. They are people of extraordinary love and peace, even in the face of injustice, disaster or loss. They are people with enough faith to give up their life here, peacefully, out of love.

Such people see things especially clearly. They are especially sure of the most important things in life.

And what do they report? They report that there is indeed a God who loves us all. That God did make us for life with Him. That love, and therefore sacrifice, is the way. And that God is behind everything that happens, and He sends whatever happens for our eternal good.

Such is the testimony of the greatest people who

have ever lived. They have been to the mountain. They have seen from on high. We can take heart that what they saw is true. ■

◘

FAITH IS NOT A FAD

Not what's in the news today.

Nothing like the songs we play.

Not like a style, a show, the "in" place to go.

Faith is not a fad.

It has been effective for a long, long time, and through many different ages.

It affects people of all ages.

It affects the same people over and over, every time they hear about it.

And no one who really has it ever gets tired of talking about it. ■

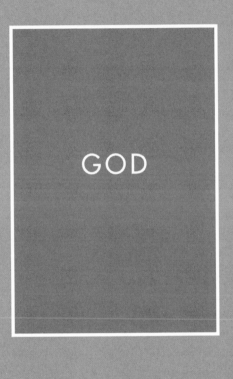

GOD

⊡

HE ALWAYS WAS

He always was. That alone torments the imagination.

He always was. That nothing should exist would seem to make more sense.

He always was. He just is. That He is, is reality.

And He is infinite. Whatever *more* we can imagine must exist in Him.

God. ∎

◉

WE ARE MADE OF
THE LOVE OF GOD

God is the one being who always was, the only one
that just is.

This means that everything else had to be made,
and still must be sustained. After all, something that does
not need to be sustained would exist apart from God.

And where God's power is, God is.

And His power is His love.

The world, therefore, and we, are made of the love
of God.

Thus, you can see the love of God just looking at
your hand. He is that close. You are that valuable. And
your life is that secure. ∎

◘

STARS AND SAND

There are more stars in the heavens than there are grains of sand on every beach on the face of the earth. Yet in every single grain of sand there are more atoms than there are stars in the heavens.

Not only does God know what each of the atoms in all of these stars is doing, but He has planned what each has done—interacting with every other—for every second of the billions of years that the universe has been in existence.

God is using all these countless interactions to create the family best suited to share His life, giving that family a share in its own creation, giving an essential role to each of its members. Of these, the earth has already seen approximately 75 billion people come and go. Six billion are alive today.

But God knows each of us intimately. He loves each of us with all His heart. Indeed, He is looking at each of us with love at this very moment. And this means you too. ■

⊡

WHY WE LOOK UP

We no longer believe that God is in, or beyond, the heavens.

And still we look up.

We still look up because, when we do, we see more. When we look down we see no more than several square feet. Whereas when we look up we are looking at as much of creation as we can see. In this sense we are looking at as much of God as we can see. At the very least we get a better sense of His bigness, if not to say His greatness.

———

Inasmuch as heaven is where God is, to heaven we also look up. ∎

◙

THE UTTER UNSELFISHNESS
OF GOD'S LOVE

As the source of all that is or can be, God needs nothing. As the source of all that we are or ever will be, He gets nothing from us and never will.

God made us for our sake only. This was an act of love so utterly unselfish that we creatures can only glimpse it. As creatures, the best we can do is work for *us*, the good of our whole human family.

And this is what we are called to do. To prepare to share God's life, we are called to become as much like Him as we can, caring for more than just me.

For inspiration, we do well to consider the reason we are here. We exist because God was unselfish, utterly unselfish. ∎

◨

DIVINITY

God made us for our sake only. He did something good solely for the sake of doing it. This is divinity in action.

It is something we imitate, however imperfectly, when we do something good solely for the sake of doing it.

This is what happens when we do what is right even though it costs us plenty and we could have gotten away with not doing it.

It is what happens when we do what is right with no expectation of thanks or even recognition.

Such acts are not easy, and they are even less easy to keep up.

But in their difficulty we can see that they are special. Indeed, they reflect life on a whole new level. However imperfectly, they are us participating in divinity. ■

◨

WE CAN PLEASE GOD

Though God gets nothing from us and never will, this does not mean that we can never please Him.

First of all, like any parent who loves us, He gets joy when we do well.

Beyond that, God put so much into our making, He is gratified by our love. He is grateful for our gratitude.

Indeed, God put so much into our making that we can interest, impress, charm, and thrill Him. He will be forever joyful in our union with Him.

———

How do we know that we are capable of pleasing God, of giving Him joy? He gave us the desire to do so. ■

PRAYER

◘

PRAYER IS NATURAL

To some people, prayer seems something quite foreign. As something "spiritual," it seems to be quite spooky, and not at all natural.

But, in fact, prayer is most natural. Indeed, once we understand it we will see that it is far more natural to pray than not to.

Let us begin at the beginning, with belief in God, who made the world.

But if He made it, He must know it. Since everything comes from God, God must know everything.

Therefore, God knows every thought of every person. He knows my thoughts. He knows that I am thinking of Him now. "Hello." This is prayer. It is thinking knowing that God is listening. It is talking to God in our thoughts if only because we can.

Of course, we also talk to God because we need to. We need to express to Him the deepest desires of our hearts. We need to express to Him to whom we cannot lie the true self we dare to show to no one else. We can do this because He already knows. We can do this because we know that He made us who we are, He loves us as we are, and He wants us to talk to Him always.

If we do, we will feel His response. In the voice of

our thoughts, we shall hear God.

This is nothing spooky. We are made in God's image. We are like Him. Therefore, when we get in touch with who we really, most deeply are, we get to know the mind of God. We get to know what He would say to us. We get to know what, through this process, He is saying to us. In the process, we become even more like Him. ■

◘

DON'T FORGET TO LISTEN

Sometimes people talk to God too much. They think that praying means "asking" or at the very least "telling." Prayer, however, is also listening.

To listen, we need to be quiet.

This means we need to have quiet, to make ourselves comfortable, and try our best to be relaxed. (Give it at least a minute.)

Now we simply, humbly ask God to tell us what we need to hear.

Soon a thought will begin to take shape. This is something we must let happen; it is not something we can make happen.

Often we will recognize the thought that is taking shape. Perhaps it is a thought that has been in the background and now is coming to the surface. Perhaps it is something new and different, and also a surprise.

In any case, this, the voice of our truest, deepest self, and also of God who made us in His image, is always what we need to hear.

Perhaps there is something we need to let go.

Perhaps we need to accept the love we never had to earn.

Perhaps we need to wake up to what we were doing and why.

Perhaps we need to dedicate ourselves anew.

Perhaps there is something we just need to see.

Whatever it is, it is always what we need to hear. It is also what we need to heed. ■

◘

"ASK AND YOU SHALL RECEIVE"

"Ask and you shall receive." Actually, this is not true. The truth is better. We receive what we need. And God knows better than we do what we need.

Still, we need to pray. Sometimes we need to pray for something. But we do not pray in order to change God's mind. We pray because, to have a relationship with God, we need to be able to tell Him how we feel.

To have a relationship with anyone, we need to tell this person how we feel. If something is on our mind and we do not express it, we fail to connect. But if we do express it, even if it has nothing to do with our friend, we feel more connected than ever.

This is the reason to pray, even to pray for something. To feel connected. To know that God is there. To know that God is God, and, according to His plan, everything will be all right.

This is the reason to pray, even to pray for something. We need to express to God what we feel. But then we say: "But Thy will be done."

"Please, God; but Thy will be done." ∎

◘

ONE PRAYER THAT IS SURE
TO BE ANSWERED

One prayer that is sure to be answered: If we pray for peace, peace within ourselves, this prayer is sure to be answered. After all, if we pray for peace, if this is really what we want above all else, we are saying that we no longer have to have the worldly things that perhaps we used to pray for. It is the longing for such things, or the fear of losing them, that costs us peace. Therefore, if indeed there is no thing we have to have, automatically we will have peace.

———

One more prayer that is sure to be answered: Often we beg God to take care of the people we love. We do not need to. God loves our loved ones more than we do. We do not need to talk Him into taking care of them. He is already at work in anything that happens to them.

He is likewise at work in us. ■

◘

WE WANT WHAT WE PRAY FOR

We pray for what we want, it is true. But it is also true we want what we pray for.

When we pray for something, we teach ourselves to want it. To pray is to look at something knowing God is watching. To pray is therefore to see things as we should, and to find a reason to want what we are asking for. This is a fact of our nature we can use. We can use it to move ourselves where we should go.

To pray for enemies is to learn how not to hate.

To pray for the misfortunate is to correct what is often our self-centered reaction to their misfortunes. ("If he dies we won't have to go.") Though this sort of reaction is often instinctive and uncontrollable, we need to do something about it. By praying for those in trouble, we can teach ourselves to care.

Finally, when we pray for ourselves, that we should grow in this way or that, we inspire ourselves to do so. We teach ourselves to believe that to grow indeed would be better.

Of course, when we pray for faith, we experience God and therefore grow in faith. ■

⊡

WHY WE ASK FOR PRAYERS

Since we already believe that God's will will always be done, why do we ask for prayers?

The answer has to do with one of the most wonderful effects of prayer: To pray is to teach ourselves to want what we pray for. Unlike wishing people "luck," to pray for them is to mean it. To pray for them is to care even if we did not care previously, and would not have cared just because we heard about it.

Thus, in asking for prayers, we are asking for companionship. We are asking others to "care with me," "hope with me."

In this everyone gains. First of all, anything is lighter if many people carry it. So we get a lighter load. Others get to love. And God gets more people to be happy if our plan was in accord with His. ■

◉

THE BEST REASON TO PRAY

The best reason to pray is this: When you pray, eventually you feel heard.

There and then you will have gained more than anything you could have prayed for. After all, if you feel heard, you know that God is listening. If you know that God is listening, you know that God is there. You know that God is God. You know that God is good. Knowing that God is good, you know that He made you not for death but for life, life with Him in heaven. Knowing that God is good, you know that He loves you, and you need only to love Him back. Finally, knowing that God is good, you know that He has a good reason for anything that happens, that He is using everything that happens to help you to prepare for life with Him.

———

The best reason to be quiet: In silence you realize you are not alone. ∎

◙

WHAT IS A PERSONAL RELATIONSHIP WITH GOD?

"I have," some say, "a personal relationship with God. It is the center of my life." What could this mean?

Faith, rightfully, originates in our deepest experiences, reflections, and judgments. It is present in anyone who has come to know that God exists. Faith becomes personal when a person's experience of God becomes an experience not only that God exists but also that He loves, that "God loves me," that "God is loving me right now."

If this becomes people's experience of God, their life of faith is not so much a life in accord with belief but rather a life inspired by love. Their experience of God gives them ongoing encouragement and guidance. Their lives have become an ongoing attempt to love God back.

———

The bottom line: Our faith is a personal relationship with God if only we realize that our deepest reflections put us in touch not with a thing but with a person. ∎

□

HIGHER SPIRITUALITY

Higher spirituality consists of a consciousness of God which comes to the surface easily, quickly, and often.

But from time to time—when the conditions are just right, when something special has happened, when a deep conversation has just taken place—higher spirituality gives rise to a "peak" experience. Notably, all such experiences are essentially similar.

Consisting of an acute consciousness of the presence of God, a peak experience also involves an intense awareness of His somehow absolute attention to me.

The experience also includes an intense sense that God has everything in His hands, and in the end everything is going to be all right.

Also, it involves a definite sense that everything is one.

In this we are given a glimpse of the life to come. At least for the moment, we would be happy to go to God immediately.

Last, a peak experience inspires profound gratitude.

Though we know we can't hold on to such experiences, we are capable of remembering them. To forget would be to waste them. ■

◘

REALLY HIGHER SPIRITUALITY

At certain levels, faith gives peace in the belief that the bad guys will be shamed, that those who hurt or neglected me will be sorry, and that all the world will know what I did, what I suffered, who I was, and so on.

As faith deepens, however, peace comes from knowing that God has His reasons, that badness is itself a punishment, that struggle is itself an opportunity, and that what we will have in heaven will obliterate all need to rectify the past. ■

◘

ADORATION

Often prayer has an objective other than God. We want something. We got something. We're sorry. In His presence we are examining our lives or making a decision.

Even meditation, prolonged reflection, often has an objective other than God. We want the facts of faith to give us peace. We want the love of God to lift us up.

What is called adoration is different. This is an experience of God, and of His love, that is captivating in itself. The joy is just looking. More beautiful than a sunset, adoration does not need to promise; it does not have to mean something.

Not a means, adoration is an end. Indeed, it is the best thing I look forward to.

Not a glimpse of heaven from afar, it is a foretaste of the life to come.

And this is what we get if this is what we seek. ∎

US AS
GOD
SEES US

□

WE JUDGE OURSELVES
BACKWARDS

Most of us judge ourselves backwards. This is what happens: We are born. We can do little more than nothing. We know nothing, and we are utterly self-centered. Yet in seven short years, more or less, we come to the point where we can conceive the idea "perfect." How do we feel? Do we rejoice because we have come so far? No, immediately we begin to get down on ourselves because we are not perfect.

As if we *could* be perfect. As if we know what perfect is. As a matter of fact, we cannot know what perfect is. Perfect is what God will make us when we die. Right now, this is more than we could ever imagine. (And the more we grow, the better we know this.) In any case, on the road to perfection we do not know how much further we have to go.

But we do know how far we have come. All of us were born as babies. Now we are so much more. It is this that we should judge. After all, it is growth that is remarkable. Grow is what we have actually done. And we should be happy about it rather than miserable about the growth that has yet to come.

——

All of us are born utterly self-centered. Life is a process of becoming just a little less self-centered.

———

Not just ourselves, *we judge our life's story backwards*. We give far more attention to what went wrong than to what went right. Though we might have done it right a thousand times, we dwell on the once we did it wrong. We want a perfect past. We forget that we are here for growth.

———

Not just ourselves and our life's story, *we judge everything backwards*. We judge our lives by what we don't have. We judge the world in terms of its problems. We forget that here on earth we will never have everything; things will never be perfect. Therefore, we do better to dwell on what we do have but could lose. We do better to notice the many good things that are already happening but don't need to happen and didn't always happen. ∎

▣

WE JUDGE GOD BACKWARDS

We judge God backwards. When we hear that God loves us, we think that He loves us despite us, despite the people we really are.

Most of us are not happy with who we are. Why? Actually, there are several reasons:

We judge ourselves backwards. We get down on ourselves because we are not yet perfect rather than being happy about how far we have already come.

All of us were raised by constantly being corrected. This, of course, was necessary. Babies have to be told if they are too close to something hot or something they could break, and being corrected is how we learn to speak. But if correction was all we ever heard, it seemed that we were always wrong.

We compare our insides with other people's outsides. In other words, we are all too aware of our own imperfection. What we do not see is the inner struggle of others.

We compare ourselves to other people's things, things they have or do. We feel bad because our neighbor has a better car, as if a car says anything about the person who bought it. We feel bad because our neighbor

is better at something than we are, as if any ability is
more important than who we are as people, as if anything
is more important than what we are as persons.

We compare ourselves with the people we see on
television. It does not occur to us that what we see has
been carefully staged to make the people we see look
good. We even compare ourselves with fictional
characters whose abilities or adventures are really had by
no one. (Who has a new adventure every week?)

We make no allowances. We rarely take into
consideration differences in ability or opportunity which
none of us brought upon ourselves. (Considering how
little some people were given, it's amazing how far
they've come.)

The final reason that most of us are not happy with
who we are is the fact that everyone else has the same
problem. Thus, we are surrounded by people who have
difficulty acknowledging the goodness in others and act
as if there's none to see.

Not happy with who we are, most of us are not
much consoled by the idea that God loves us. We feel
that this may say something good about God but not
about us. Indeed, in the idea that God loves us despite
who we are, the thought of His love may actually make
us feel worse.

But God does not love us despite who we are. God
loves us because the person He sees when He looks at
each of us is beautiful in His eyes. This is the only way
that love can happen. One cannot love what does not call

for love. (One cannot love a chair.) One loves what one sees as beautiful and good.

God loves us because of us, because each of us is who we are, someone He sees as beautiful and good. ■

◙

HE LOVES US FOR
WHO HE MADE US

God has made each of us who we are. Everything that has ever happened to us has followed His plan. It was He who gave us our starting point in life, and the struggles that have made us who we are so far.

God has made each of us who we are. He made us so He could love us. In His eyes, each of us is someone beautiful and good.

———

Does God love us because He made us good, or are we good because He loves us? In reality, both propositions mean the same thing. ■

◘

WE CANNOT LOSE GOD'S LOVE

Since everything that happens follows God's plan, we cannot lose His love. No matter what we do, no matter why we say we do it, God had His reasons we had to go through it.

Knowing this never inspires evil. Rather, if we really believe that God loves us for who we are—not for what we do—we will feel the need to love God back. And we will not be satisfied unless we believe we are doing the best we can. ■

◨

HE COULDN'T LOVE YOU MORE

Good loves each of us with all His heart. He has put His whole self into the making of each and every one of us.

This has to be true because God is not like us. We are only human, limited in every way. We have only so much time, energy, and money. Therefore, we must divide up what we give, and frequently we give more to one than to another. God, however, is infinite. He could put His whole self into the making of each and every one of us. We know that He did so because He is God, because He is good, and because He had no reason not to.

So what does all of this mean? It means that *God could not love you more if you were the only person He ever made.*

————

Another way to see it: In a world of limited goods and services, one person's riches diminish the value of everyone else's money. (If everyone is a millionaire, no one is rich.) But heaven is not a world of limited goods and services.

God's love for others in no way diminishes the love God has for you. What God has put into the making of others in no way diminishes the value of what God has put into the making of you.

———

People need to believe that they are absolutely special because they are; this is who they were made to be. ■

◘

WE DON'T KNOW WHY
GOD LOVES US

God loves each of us with all His heart. He has put His whole self into the making of each and every one of us. This is a beautiful thought but difficult to believe. After all, it's hard to imagine how this could be true.

It will be easier to imagine once we understand that we are here to become no more than the *seed* we will be on the day we die. This is a seed that God will complete at the moment of our death and bring to the full life of heaven. Then, just as a seed gives rise to something so much more than it was, we will become so much more than we ever were on earth—much more than we can imagine.

This, however, is what God sees now. God sees the future. We do not. Therefore, we do not know why God loves us. But we will. And so will everyone else.

———

Another thought about seeds: Cut one open. Look inside. We do *not* see a little flower or a little tree. What we do see does not look like much at all. It is hard to know why it is there. For this, we must wait until the seed grows into the plant. This is how it is with much that is inside us. We do not know why it is there—why we went through what we went through. But we will.

———

One more thought about seeds: The size of the seed has nothing to do with the size of the plant. A mustard seed is almost microscopic, but it gives rise to a big and sturdy bush. Some bulbs are bigger than the flowers they become. In like manner the worldly greatness of the seed may mean nothing in terms of eternity. ■

◘

A WAY TO UNDERSTAND HOW EVERYONE IS SPECIAL

Here is a way to understand how everyone is special, not just different but special, meaning good in one's own way, and no less special than anyone else. It also says something about the purpose of life.

Ask yourself this question: Which is better, a football or a basketball? Not which game do you like better, but which is better *as a ball*?

The answer: Neither. As balls, both are valuable in their ways; both are irreplaceable in their games. Neither is better.

Now this is not to say either is as good as it can be. Indeed, you can have a good football or basketball, or a better football or basketball, or an even better football or basketball. . . . But you cannot compare a football with a basketball. Each is valuable in its way; each is irreplaceable in its game. Each is absolutely special.

We can say something similar about people. Each of us is absolutely special; each of us has an absolutely irreplaceable part in God's plan and an absolutely irreplaceable place in His family. Moreover, according to God's plan, each of us will do our best. The one remaining issue is how good is our best. This has yet to

be determined. (But I will surely do better if I cease
comparing myself with others and concentrate on being
the best me that I can be.) ∎

◘

WHY DO SOME GROW SO MUCH MORE THAN OTHERS?

If God loves each of us with all His heart, why, according to His plan, do some grow so much more than others?

To answer this question, it is first necessary to point out that God's plan is fashioning each of us into a *seed* whose transformation will dwarf the differences between us now. This seed, the result of a unique struggle, will give life to a unique person whose place in heaven no one else can fill.

Of course, each of us already has a place in the formation of heaven that no one else can fill. God's plan for one is also His plan for others. After all, we affect one another. In the end, the sum of these effects is going to bring about the family best suited to share God's life.

In heaven, we are going to be together. And, just as happens here, the goodness of one is going to bring good into the lives of others. We are going to share God's life as a family. Thus, the whole purpose of God's plan is to prepare the family best suited to share His life, giving each and every member a unique contribution to the holiness that all of us will share.

Understanding the whole purpose of God's plan helps us to understand tragedy, for example, the deaths of infants. Here are people who had little chance to grow.

Nonetheless, their deaths affect many others; their deaths affect history. Therefore, as members of the family that history will produce, they will share in the holiness to which they contributed by their deaths.

Understanding the whole purpose of God's plan helps us to understand the lives of those countless people who came before us and, though they did not have the chance to have much faith, did pass on to us what we needed so we could do better.

Understanding the whole purpose of God's plan helps us to understand the state of things today. After all, look where we (as a family) started. See how far we have come. Note that progress takes place slowly, and never uniformly.

Finally, understanding the whole purpose of God's plan helps us to understand ourselves—that each of us has a part to play, that each of us is irreplaceable, and that each of us is utterly special in God's eyes. ■

◨

WHY SELF-ACCEPTANCE ISN'T EASY

It is our first and greatest call: to accept ourselves as we are, to accept ourselves as God made us.

The problem is: It sounds so easy; what could it be worth?

The fact is: Accepting ourselves is far from easy. After all, to accept ourselves is to accept our limitations. It is to accept the things about ourselves that we would like to change but can't. It is to accept that, right now, we have less than others.

This takes a lot of faith. It takes a lot of faith in God—that God knows what He's doing—and it also takes a lot of faith in ourselves. We need to trust our judgment about something that is very important to us. We need to trust our judgment about something that is far different from the way the world sees it.

This judgment is an act of our whole self.

Not so our discovery of a cure for some terrible disease. Though such a discovery would indeed be a good thing, it requires only a part of a person, and the acclaim it might bring will spare that person from having to believe in him or herself.

Self-acceptance isn't easy. But it is our first and greatest call.

———

What is self-acceptance? It is not what people think. Most people think self-acceptance is acceptance of my imperfection—being at peace about who I am *not*. But self-acceptance is bigger than that. Self-acceptance means I am thrilled and grateful for who I *am*. It means I recognize that who I am so far is who God and I have made me, the product of a struggle no less important than any other. ■

◨

HOW LOVE GROWS

It is a self-fulfilling prophecy: If we believe in the
goodness within us, our goodness comes out.

If we believe that we are good, we feel good. If we
feel good, we do good; we love. This is how our goodness
resembles God's. His goodness had to be expressed; He
made us. If we feel good, we too will care about more
than just ourselves.

If we care about others, we will feel better; we will
do better, and we will feel better still. This is how love
grows.

If we do not see the goodness in ourselves, however,
we cannot afford to see the goodness in others. The
goodness in others will make us feel bad about who we
are. We cannot love. (We can be nice to those from whom
we want something, but this is not love and it does not
last. We can do good in order to feel that we are good—
that we are not bad—but we will not feel good doing it.)
Not loving, we will feel worse about who we are, and so
it goes.

To sum it up:

Faith makes possible the love of self.

The love of self makes possible the love of others.

The love of others makes love grow.

And to grow in love is the reason we are here. It is the only reason we should never think that we are ever good enough.

———

Another way put it:

God loves you.

So you can love yourself.

So you will be free to love others.

———

You do good if you think you're good, and you do bad if you think you're bad. ∎

MORE ABOUT THE LOVE OF SELF

◘

THE GOOD YOU CAN SEE

You may not be able to see yourself as God does,
but you can see some of what makes you good and
special.

That you are special is easiest to see in the gifts—the
qualities, abilities, knowledge, and experience—not had
by everyone. (Here we are talking not about gifts that
only you have but rather gifts not had by everyone.) Of
special importance are those things you acquired with
hard work. Of even more importance are those things you
acquired seemingly without help, without resources, and
without a break.

Your goodness is most easily seen in your growth—
the qualities, abilities, knowledge, and experience—not
seen in children. Your goodness is best seen in your faith.
Your faith is best seen in your love. Your love is best seen
in your sacrifice, and in your willingness to bear. But your
goodness, i.e., your value, is also to be seen in all your
thoughts and feelings, especially the deepest.

The vastness of your value is best seen as you look
at your "self." Here, in the experience of much more than
you can put into words, it is as if you are standing on the
shore looking out into the ocean, the ocean of goodness,

which God can see in its entirety.

——

Not just another "person," what you really are is "you." ∎

◘

KEEP TRACK

Keep track of your accomplishments. Think often of what of you have already done: studies you have completed, works you have produced, victories you have won, experiences you have had, things that no one can take away from you.

Count a year as an accomplishment. After all, in a year—of work, of marriage, of ministry—you had to do a lot. Many times you had to push yourself just to get up— and often in the dark. Countless times you had to put yourself into a project, and whether you noticed or not, you made a difference every time. You helped others to live another year and grow. And you grew with every effort. You are more for all you've done.

Keep track. ∎

◩

THE DIFFERENCE BETWEEN LOVE OF SELF AND CONCEIT

The love of God where we know Him best, the first step toward a sincere love of others, we are called to love ourselves. We are called to be aware of the vastness of what we are, and the many particular gifts we have also received.

But we need to remember that these were *gifts.* As the saying goes: "There but by the grace of God go I." In other words, I realize that everything I have, everything I am, was the gift of God by the working of His plan.

But what others have not (yet) received was also decided by God by the working of His plan.

I have no reason to think myself better than any of these others.

I have no reason for conceit.

———

I do not demonstrate my humility by calling myself a sinner. I demonstrate my humility in my compassion for those who seem to sin more. ∎

◻

"THERE BUT BY THE GRACE OF GOD. . ." WORKS BOTH WAYS

The dictum "There but by the grace of God go I" is normally spoken by people in good shape in order to remind themselves that everything they have, everything they are, was the gift of God by the working of His plan.

But everything means *everything*. What we don't have was also decided by God by the working of His plan. We are called to accept this—and thus to accept our struggles, our limitations, and the fact that we made mistakes.

"There but by the grace of God. . ." works both ways. ■

◨

THE DIFFERENCE BETWEEN
CONCEIT AND JOY

Conceit follows the idea that *I* am responsible for every good thing I have or am. Therefore, I expect to get credit for every good thing I have or am.

What is worse, thinking that others see me as responsible for every good thing I have or am, I will pretend to have or be as much as I can get away with. Yet not wanting anyone to think that something was a surprise to me, I will also pretend not to be excited or even pleased.

This is not the burden of a person who admits that life itself was a surprise. It was nothing I did for myself, nothing I was owed, and nothing I will ever be able to repay. Everything I have and I am was also a gift.

Therefore, there is no reason we should not speak of things with joy, a joy that expresses our wonder and our appreciation. And nothing we don't have yet needs to embarrass us. ■

🔲

YOUR STORY IS HISTORY

It is the price of fame that "regular" people pay: Where there are celebrities, regular people are tempted to think of themselves as unimportant. Their lives, it seems, just pass. Their lives do not make history.

But our lives make us who we become. They are the means by which God is making each of us into the person we will be in heaven, a person no less special or irreplaceable than anyone else.

Thus, your story, the story of your life, is history.

———

Your story is also *His*tory because He wrote it. ■

◘

TO HAVE A LIVING PAST

Some people live in the past. Others, who miss it even more, never speak of it. Still others feel that the past is past and unimportant.

But our experiences were not meant to come and go and be forgotten. If this were true, nothing we could experience today is any more important.

Rather, our experiences are a treasure which we carry within us. (They are truly a treasure because no one can take them from us, and we will never lose them.) They are the sum of what we know about life in its richness. Our best experiences are a big part of what we can draw on as we attempt to imagine life with God. Indeed, as we remember these experiences—and as we tell again the story—we get again the glimpse of heaven that they were meant to give us.

Thus, we are called to have a living past—one that is living because it is always being added to. ∎

◻

CARE OF SELF COUNTS TOO

Because we are not God, we have needs. If we ignore our needs—because we are too proud to admit we have them or because we do not think that we are worth our care—we will destroy ourselves and add to the burdens of other people. We will have neglected the only person completely entrusted to our care. In short, *care of self counts too.*

But the care of self is not self-indulgence. True care of self wants us to need less. True care of self wants us to grow more, especially in our love of others.

————

A partial list of human needs: Air, water, food, clothing, shelter, rest, recreation, encouragement, companionship, purpose, peace, and hope. ■

JOY

◙

THY KINGDOM COME

"Thy kingdom come." In other words: "Take us to heaven now."

The basis of joy is the knowledge that we are on our way to life with God, to share divine life itself, and to do so forever.

What could possibly be better?

What could better help us to accept whatever we don't have now? After all, compared with what we will have, what we don't have now couldn't appear less important. And compared with eternity, the time we have to wait is all but over.

Thy kingdom come. ■

◘

THE JOY IS JUST KNOWING

How would you feel if you knew that you were going to get $100 million next Christmas? You would be happy *now*—before receiving any money. Just knowing it was coming, you would be overjoyed.

And your joy wouldn't last just a day. You would think about it every day; you would dream about how it was going to be; and this would be the greatest joy of all.

What you didn't have right now wouldn't mean a thing. Indeed, what you didn't have right now would only inspire you to dream.

Well, heaven *is* coming. It is better than $100 million.

You might have to wait more than a year or two to get there. But when finally your time has come, heaven is forever.

———

How would you feel if you knew the exact day you were going to die—even if it was a long way off?

For one thing, you would think of it. You would not be able to pretend that you were not going to die.

For another, knowing you had only so many days, you would strive to live each one to the fullest.

Finally, you would get ready. And you would not

wait until that last few years. You would want to make use of all the time you had. You would know you would not please God by waiting.

One more question: Why not get going, and do what you would do differently? After all, the exact day *is* coming. ■

WHAT'S TO FEAR?

Fear is a monster. It sees disaster around every corner. It sees the potential for failure in everything. It paralyzes. It robs us of our joy.

Fear does have its way of taking over. Though it may begin as fear of specific things that could possibly happen, so often it becomes that relentless fear of some unknown that is far more terrible than the worst specific thing that could possibly happen—even death.

Apart from pain so severe that it would overwhelm us, death *is* the worst thing that can happen. It seems to be the total and complete loss of everything we might have feared losing. It seems to be the end.

But the person of faith knows that death is not the end. It is the beginning, the beginning of the life for which we were made, the only life that could ever satisfy us, the greatest life that anyone can have. It is the best thing that can happen.

Therefore, if the worst thing that can happen is the best thing that can happen—and it is inevitable—what's to fear?

Giving in to fear makes a person more fearful. Every time you *don't* (do something because of fear), you become more sure you *can't*.

Heaven is a better place. ∎

◩

A GUIDE FOR THE IMAGINATION

It is possible to get a glimpse of life with God. Since life in this world prepares us for life with God, life in this world must be in some way like life with God; otherwise how could our experience here prepare us to see God? In short, life here must be an imperfect version of life with God. Therefore, to imagine life with God, we do our best to imagine life here if it were perfect—if it were all we can imagine life to be.

And let it be clear: The greatest life I can imagine is not merely life in a world where everything runs smoothly. The greatest life I can imagine is the greatest life I can imagine me having—if anything were possible.

May this be a guide for our imagination:

In imagining the perfection of our life, we must keep in mind that heaven will also involve the perfection of everyone else's life. Therefore, we must try not to imagine a perfection that presumes our domination of other people.

Actually, in imagining the perfection of our life, we must keep in mind that heaven will also involve the perfection of us. Therefore, we must try not to imagine having all we want of a worldly thing. In other words, heaven will not be an endless supply of ice cream cones—which in fact we would not really want—but rather a life where we do have an endless supply of whatever we really want.

As a rule, to the extent that we can imagine particular things in abstract terms, we can derive some idea of the specifics in heaven. In other words, in response to the question "Will we travel in heaven?" the most correct answer would begin with the question "What is travel?" In the abstract, travel is the ability to see and experience more of what is out there. In heaven we will have an absolute ability to see and experience all there is.

Of course, we must also remember that here on earth our enjoyment of anything takes place in the context of time and cannot be considered apart from the situation in which it took place. Therefore, to imagine life with God, rather than think of our experience of a thing, a power, or a moment, we do best to think in terms of our experience during a day, a year, or a season of our life.

But we must still remember that what we imagine remains but a glimpse of life with God, no more than the tip of the iceberg of what is coming. It is just a look in the right direction.

———

We will never tire of heaven. God is infinite. Not only will we know Him but we will explore Him forever.

———

Peak experiences give us a peek at eternal life.

———

If all this abstract thinking seems too difficult, you can imagine heaven by simply dreaming of the day you get what you are actually, sort-of-realistically hoping for from life here. Though this may not happen, at least you are thinking of the best life you can.

———

About daydreaming: Do it when you can. For most of us, daydreaming is not something that happens on demand. Rather, we daydream only when the conditions are right: things are going well; there is time to think about it; we are not distracted; our mind is rested. This is a lot to expect at once. Therefore, when life gives you the chance, go with it—for as long as you can. ■

◙

REST IN PEACE?

Rest in peace? Is this right? Is this what the dead are doing?

The answer is no. When we die, we are transformed. Though this transformation was once understood in terms of fire and time, it does not hurt and it does not take time. God does not need time. And those He has transformed are more alive than we are. They are not asleep.

Nonetheless, there is a certain similarity between death and sleep. Sleep, after all, is peaceful. Especially on the way in and also on the way out, we are conscious but not so conscious as to be bothered by the myriad issues that prey on the mind of every person. Instead, we are conscious only of being comfortable, and thus we are able to enjoy living without trying. This, indeed, is a glimpse of heaven.

Rest in peace? Rather, rest *is* peace. But those who have died are also in joy. ■

◨

ON THE THINGS
WE DON'T HAVE

The palatial home, the game-winning goal, the girl of my dreams: to most people, these are things they do not have and never will. They serve only to make us sad.

But the good things we see are no less from God. They reveal more to us about the life of God, the life that one day we will share. They are information that can help us to imagine life with God. And, in most cases, we couldn't have done as well without them.

The good things we don't have can serve us. Likewise the things we had but lost. So too the things that time took away. And this is one case where overly fond memories are just as useful as the truth. ■

□

THE MYTH "IF ONLY"

How often we hear it: "If only this, then I would be happy." If only I had that job, if only I didn't have this problem, then I would want for nothing.

I would want for nothing for about two weeks. To get one thing is to want another. To solve one problem is to get a new one.

We were made for divine life. Therefore, we were made to want it. Therefore, no earthly thing—no house, car, fame, fortune, or human person—could ever fill us. This is the reason that to get one thing is to want another, to solve one problem is to get a new one.

Once we accept that there will always be something, we will no longer say "if only." We will no longer suffer over what we do not have. We will not suffer envy. And, not expecting things to do more for us than they can, we can enjoy things for what they *do* offer.

———

Almost all of us understand the myth "if only". And almost all of us think that our "if only" is different.

It is different because, we say, once we get this, we know, we will want for nothing. We can't imagine what else we might want.

Of course, we should not expect to know what the

next thing will be. Like land beyond the horizon, it does not appear until we reach what we were looking at.

———

The myth "but":

"Yes, I realize that there will always be something, but. . . this is really important. . . this is for the good of other people. . . this is really the only thing I've ever wanted. . ."

But who doesn't feel that their thing is uniquely important? But isn't this always the way we say "if only"?

———

To *enjoy*, we need to be *in joy*. We need to be people of faith.

———

Happiness comes only from within. It comes when we are happy with ourselves. It is not possible otherwise. And this alone will do it.

———

A happy life begins with a happy day. It begins when we know how to be happy *now*. ■

◧

THE SECRET OF HAPPINESS: KNOWING WHAT WE HAVE WHEN WE HAVE IT

How often do we hear it: "If only I had known how good I had it. If only I had known. . . ." Yet, we remain preoccupied with what we don't have—until we have lost what we once had. Then we too say it: "If only I had known. . . ."

But we forget. We return to a preoccupation with what we don't have. And, of course, there is always something. Therefore, we are never happy.

But happiness, relative earthly happiness, is possible. It comes from turning the tables on the typical attitude. Instead of dwelling on what we *don't* have, we can dwell on what we *do* have.

We can do this best by imagining how we would feel if we lost what today we take for granted. This should not be difficult. Perhaps we have already been without it. Perhaps we know of someone who doesn't have it now.

Let us imagine we didn't have it. And how we would feel. And how we would feel if we got it back.

If we were starving, oh how we would long for food.

If we were homeless, oh how we would feel if suddenly we were taken in.

If we were unable to see, or to walk, we would tell

ourselves that if only we could see, or walk, we would never complain about anything else again.

The secret of happiness: knowing what we have when we have it.

———

Gratitude is a choice. Since even the most fortunate are often unsatisfied, it is clear that gratitude does not come from what we have. It comes from how we look at what we have. ■

◘

THE BAD THINGS

THAT DIDN'T HAPPEN

The bad things that didn't happen—there are plenty.

The times I slipped on the stairs and might have broken my leg but didn't.

The day my employer might have been upset but wasn't.

The day my car broke down *at the service station.* (When the day before I was far from home.)

If the bad thing *had* happened, oh how I would have felt. Oh, I would have thought, if only it could just be taken away.

But this is exactly what I get when I reflect on the bad things that didn't happen. These too are cause for rejoicing.

Finally, remembering the bad things that didn't happen will help us to go on when bad things do happen. We won't be able to tell ourselves that this is what *always* happens. ■

◘

ACCENTUATE THE POSITIVE

We are called to accentuate the positive. We are called to look for the good that must be present in anything God has planned.

Of course, the whole good includes the countless effects of everything that happens. It includes everything's effect on history.

Nonetheless, God being God, not only does His plan affect history but it also makes things happen for here and now. Often, there is something we can point to. A crime causes everyone to think. A fire renews the forest. Maybe the farmers needed the rain.

Of course, God being God, not only does His plan affect the world but it also forms me. Maybe I needed a day off. Maybe I needed a chip off (my shoulder).

Conscious that everything happens for God's good reasons, we can even be grateful for the hard things that could have been harder. His work on earth is over. At least you were with her. At least they never knew what hit them.

There is always something. Look for it. Accentuate the positive. ∎

◻

LOOK. SEE!

There are two kinds of people.

One sees everything in the plainest terms possible. A star is just a light in the sky. A ruin is just a place in ruins. To save a life is just another day at work. Some people can minimize anything.

Others, thankfully, see things for *all* they are. A star is a massive fireball, vast oceans of matter being transformed into energy, light, and life. A ruin transports us to ages past, and it reminds us that we come from a history of struggle. To save a life is to give a soul another day to grow, and to build up our eternal home.

Of course, to see things for all they are takes work. But the more we put into it, the more we perceive.

Look. See! ∎

◘

LIFE IS BETTER WHEN
WE LOOK FORWARD

It happens all the time. We look forward to something.
We can't wait. Finally it comes. And, enjoy it though we
might, it wasn't quite all that we expected. Once again,
hoping was better than having.

The reason is clear: We were made for divine life.
Therefore, we were made to want it. Therefore, no
earthly thing—no house, car, fame, fortune, or human
person—could ever fill us.

But, because we were made for more than we can
have, life is better when we look forward. After all, when
we look forward, we are rarely thinking in detail of the
things we can expect. Rather, we are using them as an
excuse to anticipate something wonderful. We are using
them as a way to put our imagination to work.
Consciously or not, we are giving ourselves a glimpse of
heaven.

———

If what we are working or waiting for seems far
away, we can also look forward to something in the
meantime—the summer, a holiday, the weekend. Indeed,
in the meantime, we can look forward to supper, and to
sleep. In any case, life is better when we look forward.

———

One more clarification: Faith does not suggest that we should not strive to live in the present. Looking forward does not mean that we are not living in the present. We can do both. Indeed, with much to look forward to, the present is even better. ■

⊡

LOSING LIFE BEFORE YOU DIE

For lack of faith, and therefore lack of peace, many people fail to live. Not happy with who they are, unable to face either their hopes or their fears, death or even life, they need to keep busy. When they get home they need TV. Even in a moving car they need the radio, and they need to play it loud.

Thus, they never really experience themselves. Thus, they never really experience being alive. Thus, they never really live.

Isn't it something? For lack of faith, and therefore fear of death and even life, many people lose life even before they die.

Faith makes it possible for us to live. Let us take the time to do so. ∎

◘

FAITH ALLOWS US TO FACE LIFE—
AND NOT DESPAIR

People say good-bye for good. Others say good-bye in death. Some who die were tortured. Prisoners, many innocent, are languishing in cells right now. Others are condemned to poverty.

If this is all there is, such things are outrageous. Even if it is not happening now, even if it happened only once, the truly, fully human spirit should not be able to overlook it. We should never be able to smile again.

Therefore, if we have no faith, we need to tell ourselves, "That's life," keep ourselves distracted, and a part of us must die.

Not so if we have faith. Not so if we believe in God and His plan, and, best of all, in heaven. Then we can face life as it really is—and not despair. ∎

PEACE

◘

THY WILL BE DONE

"Thy will be done." In other words: "Let Your plan for us be followed."

The basis of peace is the knowledge that everything that happens follows God's plan for our eternal good. This means *everything*—the wind that blows, the grass that grows—everything.

What could better help us to accept any misfortune or to live with any mistake that *we* have made?

What could better help us to accept ourselves for who we are?

What could better help us to live our lives without fear?

Thy will be done. ■

◘

WHAT HAVING FAITH
IS ALL ABOUT

Many people think that having faith means that if I *really* believe that God will help me, He will give me what I want. Such people are always shaken when they do not get what they prayed for, especially when what they prayed for was, in their minds, "good."

But having faith does not mean that if we really believe God will do this, He will do it. Having faith means that we really believe in God, that God *is* God, that He knows what He is doing, and that He gives us what we need whether or not we can see it now.

Many of us have an idea of faith that is not faith but belief in some lesser spirit with whom we negotiate for favors by acknowledging his power. In some cases it is belief that the mind has power of its own.

Faith in God is better. After all, God does know what He is doing, and He always sends us what we need. If this is our faith, we are already prepared for anything that may happen. If this is our faith, we already have the best thing that life can give us—peace.

―――

Some people think that if something hard happens and they accept it, the second time around things should go better. If they have accepted hardship twice, the third time things should go better. . . . But this is not faith in God, that God is God and that He knows what He is doing—even if we do not. Rather, this attitude is belief in some lesser spirit with whom we negotiate for favors by accepting what he has already sent. Faith means that we trust God even if He sends us more than we thought we could bear or more than seems fair. ∎

◻

WHY HARD THINGS HAPPEN

Why do hard things happen? The answer is always: Because God is using them to bring about something good, something that could not have happened as well otherwise, something that is going to be well worth whatever people suffered on account of it.

But since there are countless effects from everything that happens, and these extend indefinitely into the future, we cannot know the whole why about something hard that has happened. Not on earth.

Here on earth, however, we can see some of the reasons hard things happen. Sometimes a hard thing gets us a good thing, and sometimes right away. Sometimes hard things teach us a greater appreciation for good things when finally they come.

Of course, God is always using hard things to teach and form us. Perhaps, in order to form us, God needed us to struggle with powerlessness and pain. Perhaps, in order to make us struggle, He needed us to deal with life's seeming randomness or lack of justice.

What is more, in every hard thing that happens, God is giving us an opportunity for faith in Him and His plan for our lives.

If we accept these opportunities, we need no longer wonder why. We have made our own explanation.

———

We do not believe in God's plan because we can always see its wisdom. We believe in God's plan because we believe in God. ∎

◘

THE GREATER THE BURDEN, THE GREATER THE OPPORTUNITY

It is axiomatic: Life isn't fair.

Certainly it doesn't seem fair. Its breaks and burdens are not distributed evenly.

Of course, this suggests that a good life is an easy one, that the purpose of life is a good time.

But faith says that the purpose of life is to prepare for eternal life, something we do by growing in faith and love as best we can. This we do by having faith and loving, by accepting our burdens in the name of faith and by accepting the burdens of others in the name of love.

In this view, burdens become opportunities. They become opportunities to grow in the faith and love for which we are here.

And the greater the burden, the greater the opportunity. It is here that the fairness in life is to be found. ■

◘

THE OPPORTUNITIES
IN DISASTER

Disaster has several ways to lead to holiness, and even to happiness.

First of all, if disaster strikes and I am suffering something that I do not want and cannot change, I may for the first time in my life come to grips with my own humanity. Freed to see that *God* is God, I am comforted to realize that my life is safe in His divine hands.

If a disaster shatters my dreams and now I know that life is never going to be what I always wanted it to be, I might give up on the hope that I can have my heaven here. This idea, which was always an illusion, is often a distraction. If it is shattered, I am free to look to the life that always was my hope, life with God in heaven.

If the disaster was my own doing and everybody knows it, I might give up on the idea that I am this or that in others' eyes. Now I am free to see that others' opinions are unimportant.

Finally, if I was rejected or betrayed, now I have to learn to believe in myself for the right reason—because God has made who I am. ■

◘

WHY GOOD THINGS HAPPEN

Sometimes people trust in God and the patient gets well.

Sometimes someone does the right thing for the right reason and it pays off.

Sometimes a person works humbly and quietly only to be recognized later for having done so.

It will not always be so, but when things happen as they should, we are being given a glimpse of how it will be when finally we get to heaven and right will be rewarded and truth will be seen. When these things happen here they are meant to help us when things do not happen as they should. ∎

◧

DON'T LET LIFE SEDUCE YOU

Maybe you were disappointed. Perhaps you suffered a real reversal. In any case, you turn to faith. "It doesn't matter," you tell yourself, "this life doesn't last; my hope is in heaven."

Perhaps you tried and you failed. Maybe you just looked bad. In any case, you turn to faith. "It's not the opinion of people that matters," you tell yourself, "I am following God's plan for my life. This is rightfully my strength. This is faith. And having faith is what life is all about."

Two days later you try again, and this time you succeed. Now you look good. This time things work out better than you expected. Now you are back to believing that you can have your heaven here. . . or that you can do it all.

Life has this way of seducing us.

Therefore, when good things happen, expect to be tempted. Strive to stay focused on the facts of your faith.

If you give in, you will contradict and weaken your faith, and the next time you prove not to be omnipotent, you will get less peace.

Don't let life seduce you. Stay focused on *God's* plan. ■

◘

GOD FREES US FROM HAVING TO DO EVERYTHING SO WE CAN DO SOMETHING

Question: If you believe that everything that happens follows God's plan, why bother?

Notably, this is never the attitude of those who do believe that everything that happens follows God's plan. Such people know that their lives too have followed God's plan; they love themselves, and this always inspires in them a sincere love for others.

Besides, God's plan may bring about the best thing that can happen, but it does not work apart from what we do. And until we act, and things have happened that cannot be changed, the future is ours to make. Therefore, our job is to try to see things as they are and to work for what we think is best.

Nonetheless, even though the future is ours to make, even though we can make things better or worse, we cannot spoil God's plan. Once we have acted, once something has happened that cannot be changed, whatever happened had to happen—at least for then.

God would not have put us in a position to spoil His plan. He would not have left eternity entirely in our hands.

He gives us the opportunity to make an eternal

difference without giving us the unlivable burden of believing that we could make an eternal mistake.

God frees us from having to do everything so we can do something.

———

Two more reasons that faith in God's plan does not call for complacency:

We cannot outguess God. We do not know why His plan calls for what it does. The fact that it is raining does not necessarily mean that God does not want us to go on a picnic. Maybe He wants us to go and get wet.

We are here to grow. The fact that we did something does not mean that God wants us to continue doing it. Maybe He wants us to learn from our mistake and try harder to do better. ■

◘

YOU ONLY NEED TO
DO YOUR BEST

You only need to do your best, the best you can as one person, the one person you actually *are*, the best you can right now. Even if your best was lousy, it was at that moment your best. You could do no more. God expects no more. He needs no more from you.

Now this does not mean that we should be satisfied with failure. After all, to do our best is to strive for success. It is to learn from our mistakes and try again. It is to evaluate what we are doing to see if it is working, and to try to think of something else if it is not. To do our best is to try to do better.

Nonetheless, at any given moment, we only need to do our best.

———

To know if you have done your best, you can ask yourself if you have tried.

To know if you have tried, you can ask yourself what—realistically—you could have done but didn't.

And to know what realistically you could have done, you can ask yourself what others do in similar situations, especially if they have similar resources and have been doing the job for a similar length of time.

———

You only need to do your best, the best you can right now. But often it is difficult to know what the best thing is. In such a case, the principle extends to the process of making a decision: You only need to do your best, the best you can right now.

———

You only need to do your best, the best you can right now. You are not responsible for results. ∎

◘

WHEN THERE IS ONLY
ONE THING TO DO

Often there is only one option. On paper there may be more, but in conscience we know that there is really only one thing we can do.

It may not be easy. It may not be popular. It is not certain to make things better. Indeed, we may doubt that it will make things better—but it is still the only right thing to do.

Therefore, we can be at peace about doing it. At least we know we are doing the right thing. At least we know that we are pleasing God and growing.

When you are doing the only thing you can do, be happy about it. ■

◘

WHEN THE GOING GETS TOUGH

It is a fact of human nature: When the going gets tough, we want out. If, however, we get out, things will only get worse. If for love of God or others, we decide to stay, let us keep this in mind: "The problem is the reason I am here. By staying I am serving; I am loving; I am doing something good. If at times the problem goes away, let me be grateful for the break."

When you are doing a hard thing for a good reason, watch what you expect.

———

It is another fact of human nature: When the going gets tough, we find reasons to quit. They are always available. At first, most problems appear unsolvable. Sometimes others are in the way. We rarely feel we get support.

These, however, are not faith's reasons to stay or go. Faith wants to know whether it is really help we need, or is it praise? Are the others really in the way, or can we work around them? Is the problem really unsolvable; did we give it all we could? ■

◘

NOT ACCEPTING
DOESN'T CHANGE A THING

Accepting hard things is supposed to be difficult. Of course, if we have a hard thing to accept—because there is nothing else to do—it means that there is nothing else to do. *Not* accepting doesn't change a thing.

Therefore, the choice is clear: we can refuse to accept the hard things that happen, in which case we suffer, or we can choose to make the most of them because God sent them, in which case we turn them into growth. In this we also find peace.

———

Sometimes we do not accept hard things because we believe we can scare them away. This *is* the way it works in human affairs. Those who react badly are often asked for less. God, however, cannot be intimidated. *Not* accepting doesn't change a thing. ∎

⊡

GIVE IT BACK TO GOD

All too often we encounter a problem we cannot solve, someone's sickness we cannot cure, something broken we cannot fix.

Perhaps we tried for a long, long time.

Perhaps someone doesn't want our help, or will not hear the truth.

Perhaps the problem was ages in the making and it cannot be solved in much less time.

Perhaps the problem is not the kind that could ever be solved by *us*, or anyone like us.

In any case, we've done all that we could do. Now what?

We give it back to God.

With all reverence we say: "I've done all I could. You made it. If You want it fixed, You fix it. Of course, I'll continue to do what I can. I'll be open to the possibility that there will be an opportunity to do more. But that is up to You. In any case, I know that You know best. I know that in the end all will be well. I know that I am not God—and do not have to be."

If we can say this, we have turned our helplessness into an act of faith and the problem has already had one good effect. ∎

⊡

YOU NEED A SENSE OF HUMOR

What is a sense of humor? A sense of humor is the ability to enjoy the things in life that break with our expectations.

Of course, these include many things that are also terrible and therefore not funny.

Then there is a third category. These are the things that are sad in fact but not so sad in the context of eternity. They are things that we can laugh about if we have faith that God is God, that He knows what He's doing, and that in the end—if only in the end—all will be well.

We express this faith by laughing.

———

Humor is one of the best ways to provoke joy. ∎

◘

THINGS NEVER HAPPEN
THE WAY WE EXPECT

It is everyone's life story: Despite the best-laid plans, things happened that I never expected.

The reason: The world is bigger than one person. It is filled with others, all of whom have ideas of their own.

Therefore, things will go wrong that you never expected.

But, for the very same reason, things will go right that you never expected.

With faith in God's plan, this makes life exciting.

———

Never fear to hope. Since your faith will enable you to bear the disappointment if things do not work out, why not enjoy hope today?

———

Sometimes the world's problems seem unsolvable. On these occasions, it helps to remember the many other times the world's problems seemed unsolvable. When things finally turned around, it always came as a surprise. ■

◘

A TREE FALLS IN THE FOREST. . .

A tree falls in the forest. Nobody hears it. Nonetheless, because this particular tree has fallen, the wind makes a little more noise as it whistles through the forest.

One day, this noise scares a bluebird. The bluebird flies away. It ends up in someone's backyard.

The owner of the house sees the bird. He watches it a little too long. Now he is late for work.

Rushing in traffic, he runs a light and is involved in a crash.

The other driver is injured. He goes to the hospital.

His brother goes to visit him.

At the hospital, his brother meets a nurse. They fall in love and marry.

This couple has three children.

The third grows up to become. . . .

Such is the subtlety of God's plan. ■

▣

GOD'S PLAN IS LIKE
A PAINTING

God's plan is like a painting.

If we are too close to a painting, we see only random-looking spots of color. And the closer we are, the more random they look. To appreciate a painting, we need to step back.

We can say something similar about appreciating God's plan. If we are too close, i.e., if we look too intently at what is happening right now, we will have a hard time seeing God's point. When we view the plan from farther back, i.e., looking back in time and at what time has accomplished, we can better see God's hand at work. And the farther back we look, the better we can see it. ■

THOUGHTS
FOR THE
STRUGGLE

◘

LIFE WAS MEANT TO BE
A STRUGGLE

We are here to do the one and only thing that God could not do for us—to gain some responsibility for the person we will be in heaven, to become in some small way our own person.

But, for this to happen we—and therefore the world of which we are a part—had to have been made imperfect. If we had been made perfect, we would already be all that we could be. We could not grow. We could not participate in our creation.

This is the reason that we are born unformed, unknowing, and utterly self-centered. This is the reason we can be hurt, and when we *are* hurt we suffer.

All of this makes life a struggle. But struggle makes us give ourselves to the project of our life. This is what we are here for.

Life was meant to be a struggle, and it is—for everyone. ■

◘

WHY SUFFERING?

Struggle may be necessary for the purpose of life—that we participate in our creation—but why suffering? Why pain onto agony? Especially when we consider that pain is often felt by innocents, for reasons that have nothing to do with decisions they have made or something they can stop.

The reason is this: Since life in this world prepares us for life with God, life in this world must be in some way like life with God; otherwise how could our experience here prepare us to see God? Thus, when it is heading in the right direction, it is experienced as good. When it is headed in the wrong direction, it is experienced as bad—sometimes very bad.

In other words, if bad things did not hurt, good things would not be giving us a glimpse of heaven.

And if some things were not monstrous, we could not know how wonderful is the good, and how great that we achieved it. ∎

◉

SUFFERING IMPLIES FAITH

Babies do not suffer. They are not aware of their pain.

Toddlers *are* aware of their pain. But they do not, properly speaking, suffer.

Suffering comes with growing. Suffering implies a deep self-consciousness.

In its acute forms, suffering implies the disappointment of high ideas of how things should be. This implies faith. It implies that we have had a glimpse of how things *will* be, whether or not we knew it.

Suffering, therefore, is a sign of faith and depth, and even life. And no one wants to be less alive.

Moreover, once we recognize that suffering reflects our glimpse of how things will be, what caused us pain can bring us joy.

———

Having deeper desires, deeper people also have a greater need for spirituality. ∎

◉

TWO TRUTHS

God being God, we can be sure of this: In heaven,
We will discover the precise purpose of all our pain.
We will discover that what we gained for our
suffering was far more precious than what we paid—and
would gladly pay again. ■

⊡

THIS TOO SHALL PASS

The best thing about suffering is its end.

The end of suffering brings the joy of relief.

The end of suffering gives us the chance to appreciate the peace that once we took for granted.

The end of suffering gives us the chance to feel satisfied that we have endured, that we have triumphed, if only over our own limitations.

Therefore, the best thing to hold out to people in pain is the fact that their suffering is sure to end.

We can do this because their suffering *is* sure to end, if only in death.

It is not wrong to have hope in death. For one thing, we are going to die, whether we hope to die or not. More important, death is not the end, it is the beginning; it is the beginning of the life for which we were made, the life that we were made to want.

This truth notwithstanding, our suffering might end before we die. It usually does. This is also something to hope for because, once the cause of pain is really gone, our suffering is completely wiped away.

But we are still greater for having endured it.

——

Those who cannot face death think their unhappiness is going to last forever. ■

▣

ONE DAY AT A TIME

Like putting weight on a broken ankle, looking ahead in time of trial provokes pain.

Looking ahead in time of trial provokes pain by making us feel that the trial will be our lot in life. We see a whole, long life consumed by the pain we feel right now.

What we do not see is, perhaps, a surprise happy ending. What we do not see are the hours the trial will not need. What we do not see are the good things that will happen anyway.

But good things will happen anyway. The trial has no way of preventing us from enjoying most of the good things we would normally enjoy. We will not need to endure a *life* of pain. At most, right now, we need to endure only a day.

Then we get to go to bed. Perhaps we'll get the peace of sleep. And who knows what tomorrow may bring?

We can take anything *one day at a time*. ■

◘

WE ARE NEVER ALONE

We are never alone, least of all when we are suffering.

God suffers with us.

After all, God knows our thoughts better than we do. He knows our feelings for all that they are. Think about what this means. To know our feelings "for all that they are," one has to experience them. On account of His love for us, God can do no less. This is the price He pays to share His life with us.

This is something we need to know. Because it's true. And because it helps.

When we are suffering, it helps just to tell someone. It helps more if such a person appears to care. It helps most if we believe that our friend is just as upset as we are. Now we know we are not alone; and we will not be left alone. Now, with two carrying our burden, it weighs half as much, or even less.

———

God suffers with anyone whom we hurt. This we also need to know. ■

⊡

SOMEONE HAS IT WORSE

Someone has it worse. This is something we don't need to teach. Almost instinctively, people console themselves with the idea that someone has it worse. But doing so often has a limited effect because people also think it is wrong to get consolation from the fact that someone has it worse.

No, it is not.

For one thing, to remind ourselves that someone has it worse assures us that humanity can take it. If other people have endured worse, I can endure this.

Also, reflecting on the more terrible troubles of other people helps us to see that we still have something to be thankful for—things could be worse. Most often, we will see that things could be much worse and, as it turns out, we have much more to be thankful for than we would ever have recognized were it not for our troubles.

And we can be sure. Someone *has* it worse. If nothing else, someone is facing something just as terrible—without faith.

———

Dear God, as I consider the history of human suffering, and the pain of people now, I am humbled to realize that my road to heaven has been so much easier. ∎

◘

PEOPLE ARE ACTORS

Almost as bad as suffering alone is the feeling that I alone am suffering, that I alone am troubled by my thoughts and feelings. This makes me think that there is something wrong with me. This makes my suffering worse.

It is good to know that I am not the only one.

Of this I can be sure. I am never the only one. Everyone has something to work on. Everyone has ups and downs. Everyone is to some extent selfish, insecure, impatient, angry. . .

If everyone knew this, everyone would be better off.

The problem is: People are actors. They pretend they have no problem. Perhaps they feel they are being brave. Perhaps they are being prideful. In any case, almost everyone behaves this way, and almost everyone suffers more for thinking, I am the only one.

You never are. ■

◻

FACE YOUR FAREWELLS

Everything, it is said, comes to an end. The show goes off the air. We graduate. People move—or we do. People die.

In any case, it hurts; it always hurts.

In response, we have two choices:

We can tell ourselves, "That's life," and then think about something else—anything else.

We can take the pain and get the message.

The pain of any ending is a sign that we were made for permanence, for a life where things will never end.

The pain of parting is a sign that we were made for one another, that in heaven we will be reunited, never to part again. God did not call us to love others truly and deeply only to take them away forever.

To *express* our pain when there is parting is to honor those we are not soon to see again. We are making it known that they made a difference in our lives, and that they will be missed. Since this involves a certain vulnerability, it is also the choice of love over fear. ∎

◘

WHEN SOMEONE
WE LOVE DIES. . .

W hen someone we love dies, there are eight things to remember:

1. *Those who have died are not dead.* Those who have died have gone to God to begin the life that they were made for. They are more alive than we are.

2. *If you have something to say, say it.* Those who have died have gone to God. They are with God, and God is with us. Therefore, if there is something that you need to say to them, say it. They will get the message.

3. *The presence of our loved ones in God can color our experience of God.* Look for it. If you see it, you become more sure that your loved ones are safe. God becomes more familiar.

4. *We will see them again when we die.* Furthermore, we will not just "see" them, we will be closer to them than we ever were on earth. Since all of us will have been transformed, we will love better. And we will never be parted again.

5. *The death of a loved one is yet another reason to let go of life here.* After all, now we know that life here

will never be all we always hoped for. Now we know our hope is heaven. And the less attached we are to life here, the freer we feel.

6. *Grief is good.* Grief, not the lack of faith, is a most natural reaction to loss. Loss, however temporary, hurts. Like the yell that vents the pain of a broken bone, grief is that internal yell that vents the pain of loss.

7. *Getting over it takes time.* To fill the space left by a human being, possibly a life companion, takes time. Once reality without the other person sets in, it really hurts. Thereafter, there will be many ups and downs. We should not expect to see the end of the tunnel for a year and a day.

8. *Getting over it isn't bad.* Some people resist getting over grief because they feel that to do so is to betray the person who is gone. On the contrary, getting over it comes with the end of shock, the rebuilding of routine, and the gain of faith. When finally we are reunited, we will find that no love was lost. (Isn't this what we find whenever friends are reunited?)

And we will be reunited. We will.

———

Those who lose a loved one are often left alone. Others avoid them because they feel powerless to make things better. The truth is: Others can make things better. They can let a person talk about it. They can help a person think about something else. They can help to fill the void. ∎

THE
LIFE OF
FAITH

⊡

THE LIFE OF FAITH IS LOVE

The life faith is love. In other words, to the extent that we know God, we see God, i.e., we see goodness, in ourselves and others.

To the extent that we see goodness in ourselves and others, we love.

————

If people have no love, they also have no faith. If they say they do have faith, they do not know God nearly as well as they may think. Real faith always inspires love. ■

◘

WHAT IS LOVE?

What is love? Most people don't know. They mistake loving for liking a lot.

This is certainly the way most of us speak most of the time. We say: "I like hot dogs but I love hamburgers." "I love my car." "I love my house." But what we mean is that we like it a lot—for what it does for us. I say, "I love you," but maybe what I mean is that I want you, in my life, for what you do for me.

This is not love. In a sense it is the opposite of love. To love is to care about others *for their sake*. If this happens, it is a huge development in the heart of any person.

All of us are born utterly self-centered. Indeed, a baby not only thinks of itself as the center of the world, a baby thinks it *is* the world; babies do not distinguish between themselves and the outside world.

Only slowly do we grow into a new idea. Only slowly do we come to understand that the world out there *is* out there, and it is home for others who are worth what I can give them.

Actually, at first we just respect others, then, if love grows, we come to care for them, not because of what they do for us but just because they *are*.

This is love. It is interested in more-than-me. It is what makes us more like God and prepares us to share God's life forever.

———

It is not love if we do for others with *our* goodness on our mind. It is love when we do for others with *their* goodness on our mind.

———

Since to love is to care for the goodness in others, it is true: Love is a choice, not a feeling. ∎

◘

SIN IS SELFISHNESS

Sin is selfishness, the true opposite of love.

But what precisely is selfishness? Is it caring about no one but ourselves? Actually, it is worse.

At birth, all of us are utterly self-centered. We are interested in no more than our bodily well-being, comfort, and food.

As we grow, however, we come to see what is out there. What we see we want. The more we see, the more we want.

With still more growth, we come to see that others are people too. As we do, we come to want progressively their attention, approval, affection, and eventually their companionship.

If we continue to grow, we develop an interest in others. Actually, at first, we just respect others, but with more development we begin to care about others for their sake. In the extreme case, another's good becomes our own.

What has happened? We grew in our sight of what is good, and what is good drew us "outside" and then "out of" ourselves. Both these developments can be spoken of as love. In both cases we are talking about an interest "beyond" ourselves. This is really, in the last analysis, an interest in God, the source of all good, and what it wants is to be one with God.

———

A baby is utterly self-centered. Indeed, a baby not only thinks of itself as the center of the world, a baby thinks it *is* the world; babies do not distinguish between themselves and the outside world. In other words, when we are born we think that we are God. The life of faith is about growing out of this idea and into the idea that God is God, that we are part of Him, and that our hope for happiness is to become more a part of Him.

———

Sin may be selfishness, but faith is about wanting more from life, not less.

———

We do not need to choose between heaven and happiness here. Faith is the path to happiness here, and it wants us to enjoy—but also to share, and never to live for—all the good things that the world has to offer.

———

In short, sin is looking inward, while love is looking outward.

———

Sin is also shortsightedness and/or the inability to defer gratification. ∎

◘

TWO CONVERSIONS

Normally, faith grows gradually. Its growth usually consists of countless minor conversions. Nonetheless, whether we reach them gradually or all at once, we do have major breakthroughs.

Of these, the biggest two are highly interrelated.

The first occurs when finally we repent of the utter self-centeredness in which we were born. This is the day we realize: "There is a God and it's not me."

Faith in God makes possible a second major breakthrough: Faith in ourselves, i.e., love of ourselves for who we really are. In essence, this consists of faith in God where we know Him best—His handiwork in us. ■

◘

THE DIFFERENCE BETWEEN CHILDISH AND CHILDLIKE

To be childish, meaning silly and self-centered, is not considered good. But it *is* considered good to be childlike. What's the difference?

A childlike person is unself-conscious and unpretentious. A childlike person is not afraid to show interest and wonder. A childlike person has questions; a childlike person wants to learn. A childlike person wants to grow. ∎

◧

FAITH DOESN'T ALWAYS
LOOK LIKE LOVE

What faith inspires doesn't always look like love.

It doesn't look like love as parents discipline their children. But parents discipline their children so they will grow up and out of self-centeredness. They want the best for their children's whole lives. This, of course, *is* love, and what inspires it is the deep perspective we call faith.

We see something similar when, for the sake of society, certain individuals are punished, or simply denied, even though there seems little chance that they will grow from it. In such cases, love for many is supposed to be at work, and, from the point of view of faith, this is love for the whole human family.

Faith doesn't always look like love. But whatever faith inspires—whatever is inspired by real faith—is love.

———

Love is work for growth, in ourselves and others. It isn't meant to be easy. It doesn't always look like caring, the capacity for which it produces. But it is always an interest in growth, and the more the better, for more people, in the longest run. ∎

◘

THE ONLY SURE SIGN OF LOVE

Only in action do we show what we really believe. And only in sacrifice do we show that what we feel is really love. Only in sacrifice do I show that I am interested in more than just me.

There are many ways we can sacrifice: We can sacrifice our time. We can sacrifice our energy. We can sacrifice something that we would rather do.

We can sacrifice our money. The sacrifice of money is the easiest to measure. Now, this is not to say that the more one gives the better one is—after all, the person who gives more might have more to give—but we can measure our giving against our means, the giving of others of similar means, or our spending on ourselves.

We can sacrifice our security—our desire not to be embarrassed or rejected. This is what we are doing if we try something that may not succeed, or if we offer friendship that may not be returned. This is what we are doing if we try to share our faith—or at least stand up for it.

We can sacrifice our health, our safety, or our life.

In any case, sacrifice is the only sure sign of love. We would do well to keep this in mind as we listen to others and look at ourselves.

———

Time will tell. Since enthusiasm is often fleeting, only in perseverance do we show what we really believe. ∎

◨

THERE ARE MANY WAYS TO GIVE UP YOUR LIFE

Sacrifice is the essential sign of love. In the ultimate case, it means giving up your life.

This, essentially, is what the life of faith is all about. You give your life back to God, and He will give it back to you in glory.

There are many ways to give up your life. The most obvious, of course, is martyrdom. In this case, you give up your life all at once.

But it is also possible to give up your life bit by bit, day by day. This you do in any life of service. This you do in marriage when, on account of love, you "spend" your life with another person. You give up your life when you accept in your heart that things can never be the way you always wanted.

There are many ways to give up your life.

———

Nothing is more wonderful than to give up your life. Yet, if faith is wrong about life with God, to give up your life would be a mistake. ∎

◘

SO WHAT IF I'M THE ONLY ONE?

Much is not done because "I would be the only one."

It's interesting. It doesn't bother me if I am the only one who gets the prize, but when it comes to sacrifice, I cannot be the only one.

But am I not here to prepare for life with God? Am I not called to do my best, the best I can as one person, the one person I happen to be, the best I can today?

Isn't my best my share of the solution to any problem—if only everybody did it?

Isn't my love greater if I am the only one—or at least I was the first?

Besides, "everybody" will never be inspired to do it until somebody starts.

———

"Individual initiative": "So what if I'm the only one?" applied to social action. In other words, personal boycotts and other such practices which are my share in the work of changing the world. ∎

◘

YOU DON'T NEED TO JUSTIFY LOVE

You hear it all the time. In recounting a good deed, a person goes out of his way to explain it away. "Oh yes, I helped him move. He mowed my lawn when I was sick."

Is the person saying that he helped his friend *because* that friend mowed his lawn? Is he saying that he would not have helped his friend had he not received a favor first?

Surely not. Whether or not he had first received a favor, he would have helped his friend. He would have done so out of friendship, out of love.

So why the need to justify this action otherwise?

It would seem that people feel love but do not believe in it. We are unsure, or unaware, that love is what life is for. Therefore, afraid to look the fool, we justify what we do.

We would do better to think about what life is for. We would do better to notice the love we have. And we ought not to hide it from others.

We don't need to justify love—and we shouldn't. ■

◘

LOVE SURPASSES JUSTICE

A baby at birth is utterly self-centered. The baby does not recognize that others even exist.

As we grow, however, we come to recognize that not only do others exist but they are people just like us.

Now we give others respect, respecting their persons, their property, their right to hear the truth. This is the level of justice. It gets its name from the idea that doing good deserves its reward while being bad deserves its punishment. Also involved is the idea that by their actions people make themselves good or bad, an idea which is called self-righteousness.

If we continue to grow, however, we come to see that others are good in themselves, good just because they are people, so good that they are worth what we can give them regardless of what they have done, even if they have hurt us. This is called love.

As we can see, love surpasses justice. ■

◧

GOD DOES NOT KEEP SCORE

God does not keep score. He does not see us as our record, our PERMANENT RECORD, of the bad things we have done.

God sees us as *persons* who can learn, and when we do we turn a bad thing we did into a good thing we now know or now know better.

This is our power to turn bad into good. We can use it any time. We can use it all the time. No matter what we did. No matter how long we did it. Once we recognize that it was wrong, we convert it from a bad thing that we did into a good thing that is in us.

Indeed, learning from things especially wrong can bring about growth especially great. We grow more than we would ever have otherwise. This is the reason that people are often able to say: "It was bad, but I'm glad it happened."

In any case, God does not look at us for what we did. He looks at us for who we are.

———

One obstacle to putting the past behind us is the hurt we might have caused others, many of whom may still be hurting. How can we feel good about what we have learned if it came at such a price?

We remind ourselves that just as it was good for *us* to struggle with something hard, and to grow by doing so, this is no less true for others. By causing trouble, we have given others an opportunity to grow.

In the case of mothers, fathers, and friends, we have given them an opportunity to love in a very special way. After all, when we are good to others, love for us is easy. In the case of strangers, we have given them an opportunity for faith.

That others may not have chosen to accept these opportunities was ultimately their decision. As long as we have done all we could to help them—apologizing and otherwise making amends—we can go in peace. ∎

◘

HOW WE WILL SEE OUR SINS

To get to heaven, we will need to be transformed. Once we are transformed, we will look back at our sins and we will understand—why we did what we did, why we were unable to do better, and all the good God brought out of it. Best of all, from our point of view in heaven, our sins will bother us even less than we are bothered now by the mistakes we made when we were children.

When we were little children, we made many mistakes; we did many silly things. We know it, but it doesn't bother us. It may have bothered us at the time but it doesn't bother us now. We could see it all on video, but it wouldn't—at least it shouldn't—embarrass us.

What is more, the difference between us as children and us as adults will be nothing compared with the difference between us here and us in heaven.

———

Parents understand their children's mistakes. They look at their children's struggles with love. And when their children finally learn, they are only overjoyed.

God understands His children's mistakes. He looks at His children's struggles with love. And when His children finally learn, He is only overjoyed. ■

⊡

SHOULD WE EVER FEEL GUILTY?

So what of guilt? Should we ever feel guilty? It depends on what we mean by *guilty*.

If *guilty* means honest, and *honest* means we acknowledge that what we did was bad, and that we should not do it again, the answer is yes.

If *guilty* means responsible, and *responsible* means we are obliged to face the consequences of what we did, the answer is yes.

If guilty means disappointed, by limitations we did not think we had, the answer is yes. This is our motive to try harder. But, now that we know that a person doesn't have to be evil to do bad, disappointment should also be a motive of compassion.

If *guilty* means disgusted, the answer is no. Compassion begins at home.

Finally, if guilty means marked, the answer is a resounding no. God does not look at us as our PERMANENT RECORD. God looks at us as *persons* who can learn, and when we do we turn a bad thing we did into a good thing we now know or now know better. ∎

◉

THERE IS NO SUCH THING
AS BAD FAITH

Sometimes faith follows a fall. We get into deep, desperate trouble. There is no way out. We find faith.

Sometimes when this happens, people feel that they have *bad* faith. Repenting of their whole lives, they are especially disgusted that it took some tragedy to wake them up.

This is unfortunate. There is no such thing as bad faith. Faith is learned through our experiences. Sometimes it is learned gradually, through a thousand little experiences that tell me I am not God and God loves me. Sometimes we put it together all at once.

Either way, it couldn't matter less. What matters is that we learned.

———

It is not the route that matters, it is the fact that we arrived. ∎

FORGIVE-
NESS

▣

FORGIVENESS IS
UNDERSTANDING

Forgiveness is understanding.

First of all, forgiveness is understanding that no one is perfect, that all of us are born imperfect—unformed, unknowing, and utterly self-centered—and we can grow only so far.

Forgiveness is understanding that none of us had the benefit of perfect parenting, or was completely spared from confusing or damaging experiences.

Forgiveness is understanding that some of us received no parenting, or were the victims of horribly confusing and damaging experiences.

Of course, forgiveness is also understanding that, deep down, what we really want is good. We never choose what is bad because it is bad. People choose what is bad because, from their point of view, this is what they have to do to survive, to be somebody, or even to be loved—and they know no better.

In sum, forgiveness is understanding that people do the best they can with what they are given. This must be true if God is good and made us good.

But, though God made us good, we still begin life as babies. We are born utterly selfish, and ever afterwards our selfishness is often on display. This, of course, is sin. It is not good. It is unbeautiful. It is the opposite of Godly.

Thus, we *are* allowed to hate the sin, but we are called to understand the sinner.

———

People may be foolish, but they are never fools.

———

I am arrogant to insist that there is no goodness deep down within a person because I cannot see it. ∎

◻

EXPLANATION IS NO EXCUSE

Forgiveness may be understanding but explanation is no excuse.

First of all, explanation is no reason not to punish. Without sanctions, society would suffer. Without discipline, few of us would grow.

Moreover, if we speak of "excuses," we fail to encourage people to use knowledge of themselves in order to gain control over their lives. People may have had bad breaks or bad parenting, and this may well be part of the reason they struggle with certain feelings, but, now that they know, faith can respond to what they feel. It can inspire forgiveness, a right sense of what matters, or a better sense of self. It can help them to transform their struggles into spiritual growth they would never have achieved otherwise.

———

An apology is no reason not to punish. All of us are sorry that we did something that may result in punishment. But if people knew that saying "sorry" would free them from consequences, fear of consequences would not deter. It is partly for this reason that if people are really sorry, they are willing to take the consequences. ∎

◙

EVERYTHING IS FORGIVABLE

Everything is forgivable. There is nothing we can do or be that does not have its origin in human nature as God made it and in the events of our lives as God ordered them. Therefore, everything is forgivable.

This, however, is no license. Everything is forgivable—once it has happened. Until then, our actions are themselves a part of God's plan. Until then, we are called to do our best. And pressures are not insurmountable until they have proved themselves as such. ■

⊡

FORGIVENESS IS THE DECISION NOT TO HATE

Forgiveness is understanding that people do the best they can with what they are given. Forgiveness is understanding that he who hurt us is not evil. In essence, forgiveness is the decision not to hate.

But this does not mean that now we like him.

It does not mean that now we trust him. Not if there is no sign he has changed. (Though forgiveness does mean that we are open to the possibility.)

———

When we hate, we're the ones who suffer. ∎

◘

TO LOVE IS TO FORGIVE

Imagine that someone you truly, deeply love does something that is truly, deeply wrong. How would you respond?

Your response would be compassion.

No matter what the people we love have done, we still look at them with love. We still see them as good. We see them as unfortunate for their experiences or some human mistake. We are utterly open to see them grow.

Clearly, to love is to forgive.

And God, it is worth remembering, is more loving than we can imagine. ∎

◘

SEE THE SIN APART FROM
THE HURT

So often we hear of something terrible that one person has done to another and we forgive it in a flash, with some statement that the culprit must be sick; people are human; there must be more to the situation than we know.

Of course, we rarely do this when we are the victims. Then, plainly, the culprit is evil; he's out to destroy; he has to be punished.

Plainly, unmercy is the product of hurt.

This makes sense. Instinctively, we want to hurt those who hurt us.

Nonetheless, it is still love to forgive. And it is selfishness to see an offense against me as more offensive than the same offense against anyone else.

See the sin apart from the hurt.

———

Seeing the sin apart from the hurt is the opposite of the typical practice—seeing a sin whenever there is hurt, imputing evil motives to an accident, an oversight, or even ostensibly good intentions. Thus, another secret of forgiveness is to ask yourself: Did they mean to do harm? Most of the time, they didn't.

———

Seeing the situation apart from the hurt is the proper
response to almost anything that makes us angry.
Sometimes we will see that what made us angry was no
one's fault. It may have been necessary. To let ourselves
see this may not be easy—after all, hurt seeks a target on
which to take it out—but anger is not love.

———

Hurt is not the only reason for the failure to forgive.

Sometimes we fail to forgive because we want to
have someone to hate.

Sometimes we fail to forgive because we want the
person who hurt us to apologize again.

Sometimes we fail to forgive because we want to
keep another person in a subordinate position.

Of course, none of this is fair. Neither is it love. ∎

◙

FORGIVENESS IS A VOTE OF CONFIDENCE IN SELF

The hardest things to forgive are those offenses that struck at our soul, our sense of ourselves. They were those times we were treated as though we were worthless, those actions that took from us something that in our mind gave us value, those words that confirmed our worst fears about ourselves.

In such cases, forgiveness is not about accepting someone else's humanity. It is much harder; it is about accepting our own humanity. It is about accepting God's design of us rather than our own. It is about believing in ourselves by virtue of our own decision and not because of the opinion of any other person.

It is a vote of confidence in self.

Sometimes to see it this way is the only thing that can get us past our pain. ∎

◉

HOW TO LOVE YOUR ENEMY

Sometimes the goodness in people is hard to see.

It is especially hard to see the goodness in people we dislike.

It is easier if they show us. Having suffered some misfortune or fallen from some high horse, they come to us for help, break down, and bare their souls.

No longer feeling threatened, we would see such people as persons with goodness and weakness just like us. Indeed, feeling honored by their confidence in us, we would be quite inclined to like them.

Even if such people never bare to us their souls, we can still imagine a day they did, a day they fell from some high horse and came to us for help. Doing this gives us a look at the truth. After all, given the right conditions, the people we dislike *would* come to us for help. Indeed, it is likely they have already been humble in the presence of others. ■

◘

THOSE WHO CAUSE TROUBLE FOR US ALMOST ALWAYS CAUSE MORE TROUBLE FOR THEMSELVES

We are called to love our enemies and, if nothing else, forgive them. It is not easy. But it becomes easier if we notice that those who cause trouble for us almost always cause more trouble for themselves.

It is almost always true. People cause trouble because they are unhappy, unhappy with themselves. This is the reason some people are nasty or uncooperative or desperate to get their way. They have anger to express. They are trying to feel important.

This, however, does not work. Constantly embattled, they are little loved. Their idea of themselves only gets worse.

Worst of all, they have nowhere to go. We, however, can walk away. We can put them out of our lives. They, on the other hand, have to be their miserable selves every day, all day long.

Surely we can forgive them.■

◉

SEE THE GOOD THAT COMES
WITH THE BAD

Everyone in our lives is open to criticism. There is always something one can say. He's too quiet. She talks too much. And so it goes.

So it goes because so often we fail to realize that the characteristic we are complaining about is the flip side of something we would not change.

The quiet person may not add much to the conversation, but he is likely to be a good listener. The talkative person may not be a good listener, but she can be counted on to bring life to any gathering. And so it goes.

See the good that comes with the bad. ■

◘

IF IT HAS TO BE TOO MUCH
OR TOO LITTLE

Surprisingly often, we are annoyed by something that we know a person is doing with good intentions. She is trying too hard to help. He is too trusting. In terms of worrying, they care too much.

To deal with our annoyance, we can ask ourselves this simple question: If it has to be too much or too little, what would we want? After all, it *has* to be too much or too little. No one is perfect. No one can strike the perfect balance.

Therefore, what do we want? People who care too little? People who never trust? People who never help?

If it has to be too much or too little. . . ■

◘

WHO IS PERFECT?

Who is perfect? No one is perfect. No one is nearly perfect. This includes you; it includes me.

Keeping this in mind can help us be compassionate to others.

It is especially helpful if we allow ourselves to notice that we have committed sins that are similar to those we need to forgive. Such is always the case. After all, all sins are essentially similar. They involve self-absorption, the willingness to injure others in order to boost ourselves, greed, cowardice, and passing people by. All involve hypocrisy.

Indeed, once we take note of the helps to holiness that we, unlike others, have received, we may well see our sins as worse.

———

Sometimes the question Who is perfect? is posed to help us forgive ourselves. Almost as often, it doesn't work. The imperfection of others is acceptable, but ours, of course, is not. This is selfishness. It is pure selfishness—the desire to be God. Born with this idea, we are called to let it go—to acknowledge that God is God and I am not.

———

Sometimes the question Who is perfect? fails to persuade because, even though imperfection may be acceptable in theory, this person's mistake or mine is not. But what is imperfection if not real things we really do not want? To accept that no one is superhuman is not to accept anything. We are called to accept real imperfection, real things we really do not want. ∎

◘

WE ARE ALL FAR FROM
THE KINGDOM OF GOD

We cannot know what we will be in heaven. But this much we can know: From the point of view of heaven, the differences between us here are no big deal.

Here we see a big difference between saints and sinners. From the point of view of heaven, no one here is nearly perfect—and all of us are trying.

Here we see a big difference between rich and poor. From the point of view of heaven, all of us are terribly poor, powerless, in pain, and sad. . . .

The fact is: *We are all far from the kingdom of God.*

Keeping this in mind makes us less conceited, and more open to grow. It makes us more compassionate with those who might be just a bit behind us. And, if we perceive ourselves as the ones behind, it will make us less envious. ∎

▣

YOU NEVER KNOW

Y ou never know. You never know what you will do if the going gets really tough. But you can know this: If you give in, you will feel bad. Therefore, before it may happen:

Be grateful. Be grateful that you have not been tested.

Be hopeful. Be hopeful that you will not be tested.

Be good. Do what you can to show God that, given a break, you will do good. Thus, your future sin will be just a failure, and not the result of a complete lack of goodness.

Finally, be compassionate. Be compassionate to those who have been more tested than you. Be compassionate to those whose lives did not prepare them as well for a test you might have passed. ∎

▣

THE WISDOM OF GIVING THE BENEFIT OF THE DOUBT

Some think that to give the benefit of the doubt is foolish. Actually, it is quite wise.

First of all, to give the benefit of the doubt is wise because you *don't* know. Giving the benefit of the doubt can save you from rash judgments, some of which are embarrassing and some of which might leave you responsible for a terrible injustice.

Giving the benefit of the doubt is also wise because it is love. You are never wrong to hope that others have been good.

You can't lose. If you were right, you were right. If you were wrong, you were good. ∎

◉

REMOVING THE PLANK
FROM OUR OWN EYES FIRST

Wherever we share space with people, we are apt to be angered by the things that they don't do—the water jug they don't refill, the lights they leave on, and so on.

Of course, often enough, if we look closely, we will notice there is something that we don't do, that others find undone. Here we learn how easy an oversight can be.

But what about the oversight we haven't yet discovered? What can we do about it now?

We can forgive it in others. ■

⊡

WHAT WOULD YOU HAVE DONE?

The next time you feel angry about (what seems to be) another person's incompetence or lack of care, ask yourself: What would I have done? What could I have done?

If you honestly try to see the situation as it really is, recognizing the limited resources and competing demands that those responsible have to deal with, you will almost always discover that you couldn't or wouldn't have done much differently.

If you still feel there was something else that could have been done, do or at least suggest it. At the very least, remember it. Someday it may be your turn to be responsible. ■

◘

HOW "JUDGE NOT, OR YOU WILL BE JUDGED" REALLY WORKS

The injunction "Judge not, or you will be judged" seems simple enough. Do not judge others, or God will judge you. Actually, God need not be bothered. If you judge others, you will judge yourself for Him.

We start judging, i.e., we are critical, because of insecurity. Not feeling terribly good about ourselves, we are tempted by the idea that we can feel better by seeming to be better than other people. Thus we criticize. In an imperfect world, we can always find something to criticize.

This, however, does not work.

First of all, deep down, we know what we are doing. This makes us feel only worse about ourselves.

Second, by constant criticism, our idea of what a human has to be becomes harder and harder to satisfy. Eventually this idea comes back to bite us; this gives us all the more need to criticize. . . and the cycle starts again.

But we can reverse the cycle. Instead of practicing criticism, we can practice compassion.

We start by calling to mind the truth of our faith which says that we were made good—that we never choose what is bad because it is bad—that we do our best with what we were given.

We see this in ourselves.

Then we vindicate this truth by seeing it in others.

If we can do this, we will feel less need to criticize; our compassion will come more easily. . . and a new cycle will have started.

———

People speak of the faults of others in order to feel better about themselves. Once they realize this, it no longer works.

———

Compassion for self based on compassion for others might seem an excuse for sin. Such might be so if compassion for self *were* an excuse for sin—a reason to keep on sinning. But this is never the experience of compassionate people. Such people love themselves; they believe in themselves, and they need to do their best. Since they are at peace with themselves, they are more aware of what they are doing and why, and what they need to do in order to do better.

———

Compassion for others must come first. We cannot accept in ourselves what we would not accept in others. ∎

MORE
ABOUT THE
LIFE OF
FAITH

◘

FAITH IS ITS OWN REWARD

People of faith are not immune to envy. Sometimes they are especially envious of those who do bad things and seem to get away with them.

To combat such feelings, people of faith need to realize that faith is its own reward. People of faith have so much more than anyone without it.

First of all, they know more. They know where they come from. They know why they are here. They know where they are going when they die.

People of faith know that they are not going to die. They know that they are going to live, to live with God forever. They know that they are going to have all that their hearts already desire—the only place where this can happen.

People of faith know that they are here to grow in the love that prepares them for life with God. Therefore, they have a reason to make a difference in this world, and to live the only kind of life that can make a person happy.

Finally, people of faith know that God is working with them, through everything that happens to them, to prepare them to become the people they were meant to be. Therefore, they have all the reason in the world to accept themselves for who they are, to accept their past for what it was, and to face their future without fear.

If all of this were not enough, faith is the deepest knowledge that we can have. It bespeaks the deepest person that we can be. And every experience of this deeper person is, to that extent, richer. The person with faith is more alive than anyone without it.

———

In the face of human life at its lowest, the proper response is not indignation but gratitude. ∎

⊡

LOVE IS ITS OWN REWARD

Faith is its own reward. So is love.

This was to be expected. After all, we are here to grow in love as best we can. Therefore, we were made so that nothing else can make us happy. God would not have made us so that we can be happy going in the wrong direction. Therefore, when we are selfish we are never satisfied, whereas when we love we are always happy.

With love, our happiness is in our own hands.

When we love, when we are worried about other people's problems, our own problems seem much less serious.

When we love others, others usually love us.

Finally, when we love, we are better at staying out of trouble, especially of our own making.

Love is its own reward. And the lack of love is its own punishment.

———

One does not seek fulfillment. Fulfillment is a by-product of service.

———

If faith is wrong about life with God, the only life that can make us happy makes no sense. ■

◻

WE HAVE CONTROL

Control. Who thinks they have it? But, as it turns out, we can always do what we want, if what we want is the best thing for us.

We are here to grow in the faith and love that prepare us for our life with God. This we can always do—no matter what. If something goes wrong, we can accept it and thus our faith will grow. If people offend or disappoint us, we can forgive them, and thus our love will grow. When we want the best thing for us, we can always do what we want. In this sense, we have control.

Not so if what we want is something worldly.

No matter how hard I work, if I want to be rich, I still need lots of people—with money—to cooperate with me. Whereas if what I want is faith, I can get it on my own.

No matter how talented I may be, if I want to be famous—in this media-driven world where everybody wants to be famous—I still need lots of luck. Whereas if what I want is faith, I do not need a break.

If I want to be an artist, I need talent I might not have. Whereas if what I want is faith, I have what it takes, and I can also get more.

I can be a star in sports for only a short time.

Whereas if what I want is faith, I can get it at any age, and continue growing throughout my life.

If what I want is the best thing for me, I can have it. All of us are always in a position to do what we are here for. How smart this was of God. ■

◘

THE EXERCISE OF FAITH

STRENGTHENS IT

The exercise of a muscle strengthens it. We might expect the exercise of a muscle to deplete it. But, no, the exercise of a muscle strengthens it.

In like manner, the exercise, the living out, of faith strengthens it.

This happens for four reasons:

First of all, in order to live our faith, we have to think about it. We have to remind ourselves of what and why we believe.

Second, as we live out our faith, we experience the superiority of a life that only faith makes sense of.

Third, as we live out our faith, and are seen doing so, we give up what holds us back—the appeal of not taking a stand.

Finally, as we live out our faith, taking a stand at its side, we give ourselves another reason to want it to be true.

The exercise of faith strengthens it. Thus it is that the rich get richer and the poor lose the little they have.

——

The poor lose the little they have because *not* exercising their faith, *not* doing anything differently

because of their faith, they tell themselves, "Maybe it
isn't true," over and over again.

This also happens when people ignore opportunities
to speak of their faith, or they stand by and allow it to be
contradicted. ■

◻

NO GOOD WORK
IS EVER WASTED

In this age of gargantuan statistics, the little we can do often seems not worth the effort. We forget that every little bit counts—a lot.

For one thing, you never know. A small kindness can make a big difference on a bad day. A simple thought can lead someone to a big insight. Maybe the person you encouraged will go on to make an even bigger difference in someone else's life.

For another thing, in loving, *you* grew.

Even if you did not grow much, who knows what will come from a little extra holiness when finally we die and are transformed?

Considering that the fruits of the holiness of ourselves and others will last forever, it is clear that all growth has infinite value.

Therefore, even though we are also called to be concerned about the best use of our time and energy, we can still be sure that no good work is ever wasted. ∎

⊡

EXCUSES HIDE US FROM
OUR LACK OF FAITH

Excuses hide us from our lack of faith. After all, there are always excuses. There is always a way to justify not doing what is not convenient: "It's raining." "I'm tired." "I went last week." But if we really believed, what would be the bottom line?

———

Excuses hide us from our lack of love. After all, there are always excuses. There is always a way to justify not doing something that requires lots of love: "I've already done *more* than my share." "After all I've done this is how they repay me." "These people cannot be helped." But doesn't love mean that I will do all I can, whether or not they will repay me, and that I strive to see the goodness in everyone, whether or not they make it easy? ■

◘

HYPOCRISY

Hypocrisy is the basic sin of believers. We say we believe but our lives do not show it. For example:

We say we believe in heaven, but still we *have* to have that house, car, person, job. . . .

We say we believe in love, but still we do nothing that we don't have to do, nothing that doesn't pay us.

We say we believe in God's plan, but still we do not accept its work in us.

The worst thing about hypocrisy: It means that we are hiding our need to grow from ourselves. ■

◘

THE EVIL OF ENVY

E nvy is a unique evil. Simultaneously, it denies all of
our basic beliefs.

First of all, in the idea that "if only I had what he
has," it forgets the fact that we were made for heaven
and nothing else could ever fill us.

Worse than a failure to love, worse than selfishness,
envy means that we are *against* others, for the *good*
things in their lives.

Finally, since we are dissatisfied with the life that
God has given us, and bothered about what He has given
someone else, envy denies the doctrine of His plan.

Fortunately, though envy rejects our basic beliefs, to
resist envy is a way to work on all three of these beliefs at
once. There is no other way to resist envy. We need to
reflect on the fact that we were made for heaven and
nothing else could ever fill us.

Hoping that others would be happy for the good
things in *our* lives, we have this very reason to try harder
to be happy for the good things in their lives.

Finally, in order to be happy with what we have, we
need to think often that God has given us what we have

and what we don't have, and He has given others what they have, for the best possible reason.

———

Envy is almost always an ingredient in hatred. ∎

◘

WARNING!

Apart from good grief, which follows from real loss and then passes, and sadness, which is a lesser form of grief, the lack of peace is a warning—our faith is not working.

Perhaps we have simply failed to think about it. Perhaps we have failed to see, or look for, the connection between our faith and what is bothering us. Perhaps our faith is weak and we need to decide whether or not we really believe. For example:

If we feel envy or "if only. . . ," we need to check our faith in heaven.

If we feel angry about something we need to give or forgive,we need to check our faith in love.

If we feel angry at life, unloving of ourselves, stressed, or fearful, we need to check our faith in God's plan.

In any case, the lack of peace is a warning—our faith is not working. We need to do something about this, and we can. ∎

◘

WHAT IS SELF-RIGHTEOUSNESS?

Offense at other people's sins, self-righteousness, does not come from people's belief that they are better than others. Rather, self-righteousness comes from insecurity. The self-righteous have faith, but not enough. They believe, but they're not sure. Therefore, they are threatened by anyone who lives as though faith is not important and therefore not true.

The self-righteous are offended even by the repentant because they feel that the repentant got to have their cake and eat it too—that by sinning and being forgiven they got away with something.

This, of course, is never the attitude of someone who knows that faith is its own reward—that someone with faith has so much more than anyone without it. Such a person knows that the repentant paid for their sins with every second they were without faith, while the unrepentant are still paying. ■

◘

DON'T HIDE YOUR LIGHT
UNDER A BASKET

Faith puts people in a bit of a bind. It tells them not to brag. But it also wants them to spread the word. And, as everybody knows, nothing is more convincing than our actions, including those that no one would know about unless we tell them.

Clearly, what is called for is balance.

Without talking about what we are doing for others, we can talk about what "doing" is doing for us.

Without a tone of voice or words which suggest that what we are doing makes us better than others, we can use a tone of voice or words which suggest instead that we are doing our duty—our rightful response to the love of God.

This suggests that we would do it even if no one knew or cared.

And we must continue to do it even if no one knows or cares. ■

▣

FAITH IS ITS OWN EVANGELIST

Faith is its own evangelist. In other words, if people
have faith, they want to share it. This is true for several
reasons:

First of all, to have faith is to know the love of God,
and to know the love of God is to need to love God back.
And how better can we love God than to help others
know His love?

Of course, to have faith is also to know we are called
to love others. And how better can we love others than to
share with them the gifts of faith?

Of course, faith being so wonderful, we just need to
talk about it.

Faith being so important, we want others to agree.
And when they do we feel more sure.

We share our faith by living it—by being peaceful,
joyful, and by loving.

Three other ways to share your faith:

———

1. *Answer direct questions.* For example: If people
ask you what you believe about life after death, tell them,
and tell them why. If someone asks your opinion about

what to do, offer it, and explain your advice in terms of faith. If someone asks you why hard things happen, give a good general explanation. Explain that in the final analysis everything happens for our eternal good.

2. *Respond to statements that contradict your faith.* For example: If people suggest that this or that will make them happy, express doubt. State your belief that we were made for life with God and that nothing else will ever satisfy us completely. If people lament a service they must render, point out that service is sacrifice and sacrifice is love and love is what we're here for. If someone speaks of hardship as disaster, point out that it is growth if we accept it in an act of faith.

3. *Share what faith has done (or is doing) for you.* When people ask "How are you?" tell them. For example: If faith has made your life more joyful or peaceful, say so. If service has made your life satisfying, say that. If someone laments some hardship in your life, explain why it is not a disaster to you. ∎

◘

HOW WE KNOW
OUR FAITH IS REAL

If our faith is real, it should inspire both passion and peace *simultaneously*.

If our faith is real, we know why we're here, and how much God loves us. If so, we are sure to be filled with love and the need to do our best.

But, if our faith is real, we also know about God's plan. If so, we know that in the end everything will be all right, and right now we only need to do our best.

Our faith is "off" if it inspires a passion that becomes desperation because it all depends on me. Our faith is "off" if it inspires a peace that becomes complacency because it does not matter what I do.

In fact, if our faith is real we will feel passion and peace in equal measure.

———

If our faith is real, we not only view the world with both passion and peace but also view ourselves with both passion and peace. In other words, we will always strive for greatness but never despise ourselves when we fall short. ■

A SIMPLE GUIDE TO
SPIRITUAL LIFE

The simplest way to live a spiritual life: Let God be your guide. In other words, bring faith to everything that God brings into your life.

Bring faith to all your decisions. We all have many every day. Ask yourself: What would faith do? What is love?

Bring faith to all your experiences:

When you have to do something difficult, ask yourself: What is life for?

When something hard happens, remind yourself that God has His reason. If you feel down, or put down, remind yourself that, so far, you are the person God has made you to be. When something good happens, be grateful; then you will want to give back.

When you see something good that you can't have, remind yourself that you have gotten yet another glimpse of heaven.

———

A simple definition of spirituality: The wisdom to think the right thing at the right time.

———

Another simple definition of spirituality: Supernatural life. In other words, living above the level of the world, not living as if this world is all there is. ■

◨

THE MORE. . .

The more we grow, the more we know.

The more we know, the more we love.

The more we love, the more we become like God.

———

The more we become like God, the better we know Him.

The better we know God, the more we want to be with Him.

The more we want to be with God, the less attached we are to anything on earth.

———

The more we become like God, the better we know His mind.

The better we know God's mind, the better we understand His plan.

The better we understand God's plan, the better we see His plan at work.

The better we see God's plan at work, the more we feel at peace.

———

The more we become like God, the better we know His mind.

The better we know God's mind, the better we know His will—what He would do in any situation.

———

The more we become like God, the more we feel His love.

The more we feel God's love, the more we want to please Him—and the less we feel we have to.

———

The more we become like God, the more like God we see.

The more like God we see, the better we see the good in others.

The better we see the good in others, the more we want to give, and the more we can forgive.

———

The more we become like God, the more we love ourselves.

The more we love ourselves, the more we love others.

The more we love others, the more we become like God. ■